STRATEGIC DRIVEN LIFE

WORKBOOK / JOURNAL

STRATEGIC DRIVEN LIFE

WORKBOOK / JOURNAL

WITH DISCOVERY GROUPS

2nd Edition

A COURSE IN VISIONARY STUDIES

DR. E. DEREL PETERSON

FOR SDL RESOURCES CONTACT:
World Class Leadership SDL
edp@worldclassleadershipsdl.com

Copyright © 2024 by Edward Derel Peterson

Copyright TX9-424-661
Paperback ISBN: 979-8-9925153-3-6
Hardcover ISBN: 979-8-9925153-4-3

TRIBUTE

In tribute to my father, L. D. Peterson,
the most extraordinary man I've ever known!

VISIONARY PHILOSOPHY

If anyone knows anything about the love of God
They know something about the love of all humanity.

And in that Love, *THE WINNER* emerges …
Become who you want to be
for in the end
the only thing that will be
is who you have become

Afterwards
Nothing goes with you but who you are
and nothing left behind
rivals the absence of who you have been

"I am not what happened to me, I am what I choose to become"
"The world will ask you who you are, and if you do not know the world will tell you."
"The privilege of a lifetime is to become who you really are."

CARL JUNG

TABLE OF CONTENTS

MASTER THE STRATEGIC DRIVEN LIFE

VISIONARY PREFACE

Scientists have our respect and deep appreciation for their enormous achievements. Religionists have our respect as they try to unravel the mysteries science cannot directly address. Yet, there is an understandable debate between science and religion. Though scientists and religionists have similar aims of embracing the truth, their constructs of existence and methods of interpretation are essentially distinct. The challenge of reconciling their findings is difficult, though there seems to be some attempt at achieving this goal.

Though this Strategic *Driven Life Visionary Design* is not engaged in that contest, it supports a complementary approach toward an integrated understanding of the two fields. Instead, the *Strategic Driven Life* approach articulates the implications of human origin and life experiences.

Since neither science nor religion can definitively conclude origins particulars, human origin becomes a matter of personal choice regarding individual determination. Because of its practical implications for life, this decision is more about the future than the past.

This writing focuses on the life we experience as human beings on planet Earth. This life is directly affected by the massive implications of human origin. In this choice, humans discover their domain of existence, core identity, and the perimeters of human experience. These comprehensions provide a consequential impact on the visionary future of humanity. Your vision of the future becomes the maturation of your view of the past. Fortunately, you can holistically define your past today by selecting your human origin through a simulated time travel approach. Go to the past to see your future.

The *Strategic Driven Life* (SDL) approach envisions your life and its future as the implications of your choice of human origin. Life and origin are essentially related. Just as a child born of its human parents is a projection of their image. It is a demonstration of the essential relationship between birth and life experiences. Similarly, human origin naturally determines the life of its birth. That is, what it is like to be human.

Origin determines your Domain of Existence. Subsequently, your chosen domain of origin specifies what you are (DOE, existence), why you exist (COG, cause), who you are (COB, expression), and how you will live (MOC, experience). In aligning these four components, existence, cause, expression, and experience, your life possesses holistic compositional integrity and fulfillment. It's the life your origin offers.

Without essential alignment, your life is an unfulfilled and confused piecemeal exercise. When existence (what you are), expression (who you are), and experience (how you live) are not consistent, life is not complete. Again, this alignment dynamic is not a debate between science and religion but simply a rational application of essential components of human existence and reality. The best and most fulfilled life aligns all three into perfect harmony.

Human origin and life possibilities are your decision. It's your choice. It's your life. You decide!

It is my privilege to be your guide in this visionary process. I will do my best to facilitate your journey with respect, due deliberation, and as much neutrality as I can muster. Since I have opinions, some measure of inference may appear.

Very Best wishes!

VISIONARY INTRODUCTION

A vision is more than a wish. It is more than inspiration or aspiration. Yet, any beneficial vision contains both aspiration and inspiration. A vision is a hope-filled future. Yet, it brings more than hope provides. In strategic designs, a vision brings clarity and certainty regarding future passions and possibilities. Your vision is about who you want to become as the basis for what you want to achieve. A good vision accelerates your performance, affirms who you want to become, and amplifies your spirituality. The SDL visionary system engages three modules to facilitate the design of a good vision: elevating your potential, designing the person you want to become, and defining the spirituality that defines you.

Your vision embraces life in all its parameters, integrated into a journey of significance that provides meaning. A compelling vision is the projection of a designed intentional future with clarity, strategy, passion, reality, purpose, performance, and hope.

The strategic-driven life visionary design employs Ideas of Significance for a Life of Magnificence! The significance of the ideas that drive you determines the brilliance of the life you experience. Ideas give vision the Power to Perform.

Significant ideas give meaning to the human journey. They define the essence of human existence as the Domain Of Existence (DOE), the reason for our being as the Center Of Gravity (COG), the human expression as the Core Of Being (COB), and the range of human experience as the Master Of Ceremonies (MOC). They provide an overarching understanding of human origin and its characteristics translated into your life and future.

Significant ideas are holistic, not fragmented. When ideas of division and brokenness fill the world, humanity suffers greatly, and rulers gain absolute power. Magnificent life is lost. Death reigns supreme. Brokenness becomes universal. Build a vision with significant ideas of wholeness and make the world beautiful, beneficial, and peaceful.

Significant ideas are influential. They shape the way we think and live. Governments submit to their dominance, cultures to their expressions, and societies to their thoughts. With the power of ideas, we design the world. That's why ideas are crucial. They must historically stand the test of time and demonstrably produce human benefit.

This visionary studies course employs significant ideas as essential components of imaginative design. These design elements enable *Strategic Driven Life* readers to build a vision with the power to perform beyond the capacity to envision.

STRATEGIC DRIVEN LIFE GUIDANCE

If life's journey is to be intentional rather than happenstance, guidance is an essential key to success. Guidance is akin to wisdom. Wisdom is linked to the acquired benefits of counsel. And counsel is itself an expression of guidance. The SDL design guides with Intentionality. In its Circle of Intentionality, the Strategic Driven Life text engages several kinds of guidance: conceptual, strategic, empowerment, and behavioral.

- Conceptual Guidance – Universal ideas regarding the human condition
- Strategic Guidance – The most critical dimensions of life over the entire tenure of life
- Empowerment Guidance – To empower in direction is to guide in life's destiny
- Behavioral Guidance – Introduce significant ideas into human behavior

Conceptual Guidance: Generally accepted ideas regarding the human condition

1. Vision is a glory-driven strategic strategy
2. Phenomenal human growth potential
3. Human Performance builds on responsibility
4. Humanity's center of gravity
5. Shaping human passion
6. Elevate human intelligence
7. Defining human spirituality
8. Sacred spirituality determines the future
9. Wholeness as Humanity's Theory of Everything
10. Culture serves as the basis of peace
11. Stewardship matures influence

Strategic Guidance: Engages the most important dimensions of life over the entire tenure of life.

1. Strategic guidance format – A glory-driven life strategy
2. Your potential is dynamic – Expansions beyond constrictions
3. Your runway of accelerating performance – Authorized living
4. Your Center of Gravity is a choice – It holds everything together
5. You create life inspirations – Pulsating passions form an inscribed heart
6. Your mind thinks what your chosen glory speaks – Thoughts your mind hears
7. Your chosen glory defines your spirituality – Life's meaning
8. Your sacred values determine your future – Sacred conditions create tomorrow

9 . In chosen glory, your life becomes broken or whole – Holy Oneness

10. Build relationships into partnerships – Partnerships into culture

11 . Stewardship matures influence

Guidance from Eleven Life Empowerments

1 . Celebrate calculated achievements.

2 . Stretch in the Beyond Arena.

3 . Assume responsibility for life and mission.

4 . The power of choice.

5 . Passion from an inscribed heart.

6 . Listen to the music…

7 . Wind beneath your wings.

8 . Value the Sacred

9 . The power of one.

10. Exponential power levels.

11. The power in your serve.

Guidance from Eleven Behavioral Objectives

1 . Build your SDL vision as an intentional, empowered, glory-driven life, strategy

2 . Become more than you can be.

3 . Become a person of maturing distinction.

4 . Become a person of value with meaning and purpose.

5 . Write in your heart your chosen glory characteristics as the core of who you are

6 . Design your mind (hear/learn/think) as the intelligent thought your glory conveys

7 . Become the glory-driven spirituality that defines you.

8 . Give your world a great future – Value the sacred imperative.

9 . Become an instrument of Peace in Holy Wholeness.

10. Build a beyond culture of partnerships in love, light, and life

11 . Maximize stewardship that matures influence

STRATEGIC DRIVEN LIFE PERFORMANCE
Power Performance System (PPS)

The Visionary Power Performance System (PPS) enables a vision of significance to become a reality. It is the power to perform. A vision creates objectives with design and intent. Yet performance requires enablers that empower the design to actualize its intended purpose. There are seven powers to perform that facilitate this process. They are determinations of discernment, pathways of direction, concepts of knowledge, accelerations of potential, domains of motivation, characterizations of spirituality, and avenues of progress—these powers of performance help to build a Vision of Significance for a Life of Magnificence. Read on – to dream on!

These powers to perform are found in various expressions throughout the book. When reading the SDL text, make PPS notes with letter markings indicating the power embraced. Each power category is notated by its highlighted letter(s). This recording process enables the reader to note important ideas and categorize them for empowerment in one's journey.

- The Power of Choice – Determinations of Discernment
- The Power of Direction – Pathways of Leadership
- The Power of Knowledge – Concepts of Intelligence
- The Power of Spirituality – Characterizations of Meaning
- The Power of Potential – Accelerations of Maturity
- The Power of Motivation – Domains of Passion
- The Power of Progress – Avenues of Achievement

1. The Power of Choice—Determinations of Discernment—The life you live is the life you choose. Yet, life is not about absolute perfection but continuous movement in life's discerning direction. In your Power of Choice, you may select your strategic framework of holistic living, as presented in the Strategic Driven Life text and workbook.

2. The Power of Direction – Pathways of Leadership – Direction is the self-evident act of leadership. To lead is the ability to make decisions that chart a course of action – a pathway to the future. You can only lead when you know where you are going. Direction is vital – it's your choice at your discretion. The further distance your direction encompasses, the greater the influence your leadership provides.

3. The Power of Knowledge – Concepts of Intelligence – Knowledge as the objective of information produces systems of thought for intelligence and life. Knowledge as understanding defines and guides the human journey. The Bible emphasizes its importance: "My people perish for lack of knowledge." There is a significant distinction between life with or without understanding. Knowledge is critical to an effective life. Examine each chapter for concepts of knowledge that will facilitate your journey. Record those you find meaningful and helpful. As you apply them in your life, they become the power of knowledge to perform – intelligently.

4. The Power of Spirituality – Characterizations of Meaning – reconciles why you exist (purpose), who you are (meaning), and how you live (behavior) – personal wholeness. One's purpose and meaning are discovered in spirituality, which translates to performance. Power Concepts of Spirituality aim to produce human wholeness as transcendent and significant ideas that contribute to building your magnificent life. They are meaningful thoughts of a glory-driven spirituality that will help you accomplish your Behavioral Objective. Therefore, define the spirituality that defines you. Make sure it is sufficient for the challenges of this world and beyond. Consume spirituality as the essence of your life – It is! Specify the power of spirituality as found in the last five chapters and record the ideas that formulate and facilitate its presence in your life.

5. The Power of Potential – Accelerations of Maturity – Potential is dynamic. Its capability is achieved in maturity. Your potential is, therefore, a matter of continual growth toward maximizing your capabilities. Grow and become more than you can be. Potential and maturity are found explicitly in chapters two and three. Study and record ideas that facilitate their presence in your journey. Mature as a person and grow into more than you can be. Learn the process of maturity and potential.

6. The Power of Motivation – Domains of Passion – Without motivation, people stop moving. That's why the Strategic Driven Life is filled with the empowerment of motivation. Keep Going! Build a vision worth living and be passionate about the journey. Employ empowerments, forward movers, and the complete power performance system. Be empowered for a journey that matters in a vision you design. Record the sources of empowerment in each chapter. Apply them to your life.

7. The Power of Progress – Avenues of Achievement – Goals are avenues of achievement. When your goals are achieved, success is acquired, and progress is realized. Keep making progress one step at a time. Keep moving forward. Choose your goals and make them happen. Progress is an achievement, and achievements are fun. Employ Fun Power. Celebrate success! Record your goals and celebrate your progress in achieving them.

MASTER THE STRATEGIC-DRIVEN LIFE TEXTBOOK

(Please note the SDL ELE textbook's "Chapter Reading Guide" is presented below to assist the reader with mastering its content.)

- Read the SDL Introduction – note key ideas.
- Read the SDL book "11 Chapter Openings" through the Behavioral Objective to grasp the theoretical intent of each chapter's content . In your notes, specify each chapter's intent or purpose and key elements that help make it happen .
- Create DISCOVERY GROUPS for accelerating Aligned Human Potentials through:
  - Humanity's Domain Of Existence – DOE
  - Humanity's Reason For Being – COG
  - Humanity's Expression of Identity – COB
  - Humanity's Experiential Journey – MOC
  - Humanity's Envisioned Future – Vision of Life Possibilities
  - Discover Ideas of Significance for a Life of Magnificence

> ▶ *ACTION ITEM ONE: Read the eleven "Chapter Openings or Theoretical Intents" in the SDL ELE book, concluding with the Behavioral Objective. Give special consideration to the chapter's intent or purpose, as clearly stated in the opening portion of the chapter. Share one or more of the intentional emphasis you find most helpful with your Discovery Group.*

- Read and make Power Performance System (PPS) notes on the First Module (Chapters 1-3). Read, the entirety of each chapter, making PPS notes as appropriate. Carefully consider the Chapter's, Opening Intent and Chapter Storyline – Intent Illustrations – Elevate Your Potential.

> ▶ *ACTION ITEM TWO: Read chapters 1-3 in their entirety, paying particular attention to the Storyline illustrations of Applied Theoretical Intent for Elevating Your Potential. Discover illustrations of intentional behavioral characteristics that accelerate your potential. Share beneficial behavioral illustrations from your PPS chapter notes with your Discovery Group.*

- Read and make PPS notes on The Second Module (chapters 4-6), "Chapter Storyline – Intent Illustrations"– Design the Person You Want to Become .

▶ *ACTION ITEM THREE: Read chapters 4-6 in their entirety, paying particular attention to the Storyline Illustrations of Applied Theoretical Intent for Designing the Person You Want to Become. Discover illustrations of intentional behavioral characteristics that help design your dream person. Share beneficial behavioral illustrations from your PPS chapter notes with your Discovery Group.*

• Read and make PPS notes on The Third Module (chapters 7-11), "Chapter Storyline – Intent Illustrations" – Define the Spirituality That Defines You .

▶ *ACTION ITEM FOUR: Read chapters 7-11 in their entirety, paying particular attention to the Storyline Illustrations of Applied Theoretical Intent for Defining the Spirituality That Defines You. Discover illustrations of intentional behavioral characteristics that help define your spirituality. Share beneficial behavioral illustrations from your PPS chapter notes with your Discovery Group.*

Now that you have gained mastery of the Strategic Driven Life textbook, you are ready to specify and embrace your Glory Driven Life Strategy and Master of Ceremonies' Glory Empowerments as outlined in pages 11-18. This amplifies your understanding of your Origin-defined person and your Origin's Glory Empowerments for identifying, shaping, and energizing who you choose to become.

STRATEGIC DRIVEN LIFE STRATEGY

The Strategic Driven Life visionary design employs *ideas of significance for a life of magnificence*! Ideas give vision the capability of producing a life worth living with the power to perform its intentionality of purpose.

Perhaps the most fundamental and transcendent idea of human existence relates to its origin and associated characteristics of glory. Human origin determines human existence. Human existence determines human life. In life, we meet destiny.

Human origin is not just your starting point. It's who you are. It's not just where you began. It's where you are going. Your choice of origin will determine your Center of Gravity (COG), your Core of Being (COB), and the Master of Ceremonies (MOC) for your life.

Origin is the hub around which all else revolves. In your choice of origin, the future becomes the maturation of your past. Science and religion give input, but questions remain. It's your life. It's your choice. It's your future.

Acquire a clear understanding of each human origin option and its absolute world-shaping powers. Your choice of human origin affects everything. It will produce human spirituality, and human spirituality will shape the world. The twentieth century was a profound example of these influences, and the twenty-first century will accelerate the influence of human origin. The following Glory-driven Life Strategy Diagram helps to illustrate the impact of your choice of origin.

STRATEGIC DRIVEN LIFE
Glory Driven Strategy Diagram

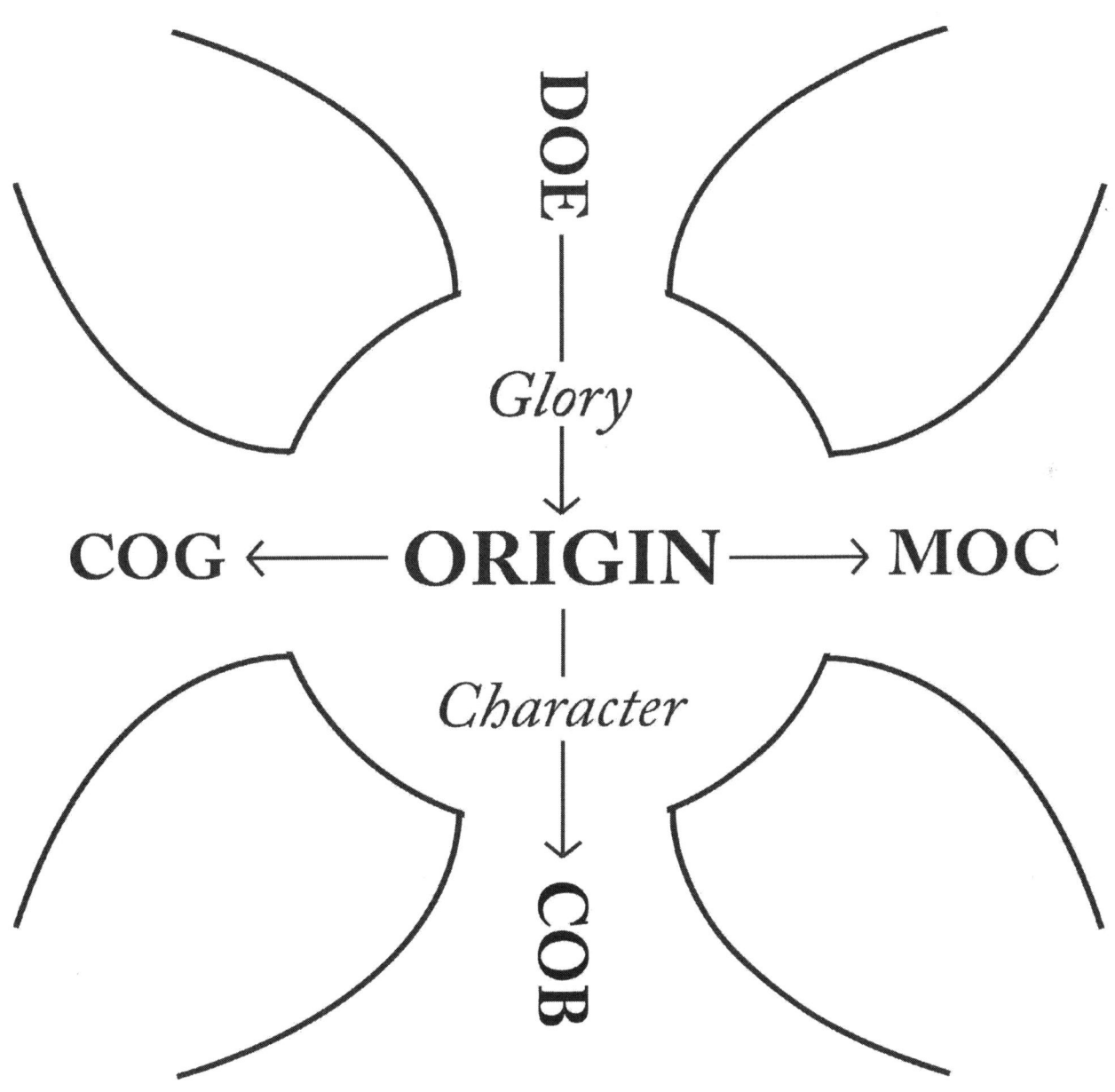

LEGEND
DOE—DOMAIN OF EXISTENCE – What you are
COG—CENTER OF GRAVITY – Why you exist
COB—CORE OF BEING – Who you are
MOC—MASTER OF CEREMONY – How you live

The above Glory-driven Life Strategy Diagram illustrates the power of one's choice of human origin as it relates to what we are (DOE), why we exist (COG), who we are (COB), and how we live (MOC). These dynamics generate your life, journey, and destiny.

Experience is the most powerful, exhilarating, impacting exercise of human existence. In experience, reality becomes tangible, amplified, and illustrated in the human arena. In experience, we taste, touch, smell, hear, and see the observable world. It's a vital part of the scientific methodology. Experience attempts to disseminate discoveries of reality throughout the human personality. It reconciles human understanding into one realized, actualized component. Instead of a reality of brute facts, the experience turns truth into brilliant portraits of realized dimensions. Considering the powerful array of human experience, the MOC glory characteristics offer profound transformational capabilities for human enlightenment, advancement, and fulfillment.

The MOC experience is the avenue by which the DOE glory characteristics influence the human condition. MOCs merge the glory characteristics of their domain with the human personality regarding spirituality, rationality, development, and human relational capabilities. Embraced MOCs determine how you live and the progress you make.

▶ *ACTION ITEM FIVE: Discuss the Glory-Driven Life Strategy Diagram with your Discovery Group. Share your thoughts regarding how these concepts may influence your future.*

As we affirm with devotion the glory characteristics of the creator, cosmos, or both, we *value* their prominence in the fullness of who they are and how they function – adoration/worship. As we *live* and emulate their character and function, we become a demonstration of who they are – lifestyle/ discipleship. As we absorb or ingest the cosmic or Creator/cosmic glory characteristics, we *become* their glory in human flesh – living expressions of personal likeness.

The MOCs become our lives' central guiding and empowering passion in adoration of worship, a lifestyle of discipleship, and characteristics of likeness. In this process of worship, discipleship, and likeness, MOCs are inscribed or written in your heart. These MOCs of God's Glory of Character become a *Character-Driven Glory Discipleship*. Let God's Glory disciple your life. What you write in your heart determines who you become. This inscribed heart shapes you by writing its MOC likeness, knowledge, and transforming influence in you. "For as he thinketh in his heart, so is he." (Proverbs 23:7)

Moses, one of the most influential leaders in human history, knew the power of the MOC experience. Perhaps his MOCs made Moses who he was. His passion was to behold the glory of God in deep adoration (Ex 33:18-19). God's glory became the guiding, passionate MOC for Moses' life and journey. Moses was significantly affected by the experience of God's glory. His face glowed from living in the glory of God. In his MOC of God's glory, he experienced God's manifest presence, knowledge, and transformation.

Moses became a glowing expression of God's glory – presence. The bearer of God's thoughts in the Ten Commandments – revelation knowledge. And the leader of nations past and future – transformation. The abiding presence of MOC glory characteristics suggests the ordinary should be concerned (look out), for the extraordinary may become commonplace.

Please note that when you employ an MOC by inscribing it in your heart, you experience its essence and become its likeness. Furthermore, you gain access to the insight or knowledge the MOC possesses. MOCs possess knowledge that is possibly hidden in their definition but revealed to the glad recipient of their character. In this cumulative effect, they transform your life and world. Indeed, your world becomes the tributary of the MOC that inscribes your journey. That tributary may become a massive river that reshapes your life's terrain at any time. The land you once knew may become a domain you have not experienced. Look out; the ordinary has become extraordinary, and the world has changed significantly. Value the MOCs that inscribe your life, for their reality, defines your destiny.

Though its *Cosmic Glory* is magnificently vast, yet finite, of limited impact, and with minimal capabilities, perhaps its MOC characteristics provide the same results regarding presence, understanding, and change. MOCs convey to those who embrace its domain of glory all its capabilities in the experience of presence, knowledge, and potential. MOC cosmic glory offers magnificence, beauty, complexity, symmetry, fascinating configurations, weird, wild, phenomenal operational functions, human progression, and futures, to name a few. Yet its cosmic cry is always the same – nothing special, just accidental, ordinary, limited, and restricting terminal matter. As wonderful as these glorious characteristics may be, humans may need more than they can provide to experience life beyond the sun and radiant life on planet Earth.

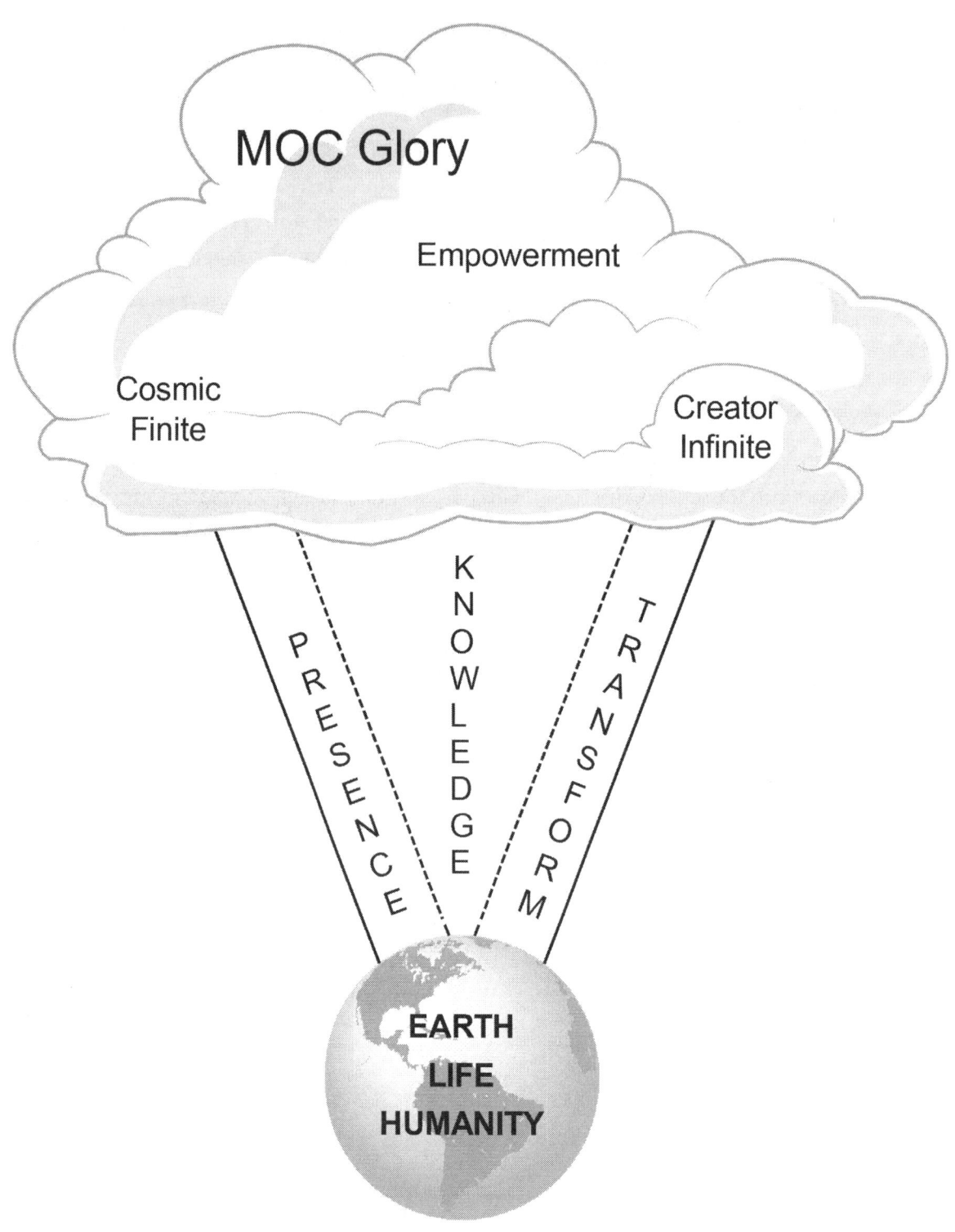

Three Categories of Glory Characteristics

There are three categories of glory characteristics: causal, emulative, and intentional. They translate into three types of MOCs. *Causal MOCs* are power or authoritative characteristics. *Emulation MOCs* are exemplary for shaping human behavior. *Intentional MOCs* are destiny characteristics for all elements within their sphere. Causal or power MOCs are transformative. Emulation or behavioral MOCs are informative. Intentional MOCs are determinative. MOC glory characteristics are not limited to any category and may have multiple dimensions of these possibilities.

When projecting your future aspirations or vision, you may reach for anything you want, but you can only experience what your chosen domain of glory possesses and thereby provides. Origin's domain is determinate. Existence dictates or determines – essence, expression, and experience.

For humans, a disconnect from their chosen reality (COG) occurs when experience exceeds existence. Your chosen COG defines your reality. It is the universal and contextual domain in which you live. If you choose to live or experience that which your chosen glory does not possess, you have moved beyond its domain. Therefore, you need to rethink your choice of human origin. Your domain of existence is your domain of life.

Remember, you can only experience what your chosen glory possesses. When your experience matches your chosen glory, you manifest personal integrity as to your chosen origin of life. For scientists, this scientific challenge requires that all cosmic experiences align with their material substance and origin. Similarly, the religious encounter the same obstacle as they attempt to align all things to their spiritual construct of existence and origin. In this combination of aligned character and experience, fulfillment is achieved.

To experience something contrary to its glory expressions is to embrace characteristics beyond its domain and imply origin beyond its essence. This violation between essence and experience brings brokenness between what you are and what you experience. Thereby, life is deficient, unfulfilled, and without completion – broken. A life of wholeness requires uniformity of alignment between essence/what, expression/who, and experience/how.

The glory characteristics you select as your MOCs will empower your vision. They will also guide and enable your life decisions, directions, and lifestyle. They equate essence, existence, and experience. Follow your guides!

Three Windows of Glory Characteristic Influence

Consider three windows of glory characteristic influence in making your decision regarding human origin with its guides and empowerments. The *first window of glory characteristic influence* is its impact on *individual life*. Chapter four in the SDL text illustrates this dynamic by addressing characteristics of both human origin options. These two domains of origin determine human identity, life, and destiny. They define human existence, essence, expression, and experience . They produce the inherent characteristics of the glory-driven life . In this workbook, the two Glory-Driven Chart Models illustrate the characteristic influences of each choice .

The *second window of glory characteristic influence* this human choice of origin provides relates to its *corporate impact on humanity.* That is its profound influence on spirituality and corporate influence on the entire human race. Spirituality creates culture. Culture produces society. Society becomes the nation. Nations become the world. Chapter seven on spirituality, as found in the SDL text, illustrates this powerful world-shaping influence. The last four chapters also contribute to this window of corporate spiritual influence.

The *third window of glory characteristic influence* suggests that the real challenge for humanity's future on planet Earth is its *ability to produce effective people.* That is, people who can voluntarily get along with one another in discerning judgment and sound mental health. This human opportunity of harmony equates to peace on earth. Otherwise, powerful governments decide human existence with brutal regimes of absolute tranny, and the possibility of total world destruction is within reach. As chapter eight demonstrates, spirituality is the key to this corporate human characteristic of sound mental health in love or hate, peace or war. Choice of origin shapes universal human spirituality and destiny.

With their glory characteristics, the cosmic and the Creator/cosmic domains of existence determine human experience. The Creator/comic domain generates its ultimate inherent glory in the manifestation of life. Meanwhile, the cosmic domain, by definition, generates its ultimate glory of material finality in death. The Creator/cosmic domain is characterized by everlasting life beyond the material world. The cosmic domain is characterized by its rejection of anything beyond the material realm and, therefore, embraces its inherent material terminal domain of death that is eternal. You receive your characterizations of the human journey in your choice of human origin. The relationship between existence and experience is the basis for this Strategic Driven Life system projecting the human life journey and destiny.

> ▶ *ACTION ITEM SIX: What benefits do you envision from employing the MOC Glory Empowerments? Share your empowering insights on the MOC GLORY LIFE EMPOWERMENT DIAGRAM with your Discovery Group.*

On pages 20 – 25, you will discover the Cosmic Glory Driven Life Strategy as displayed in the Cosmic Chart of Human Origin. This Chart amplifies your cosmic glory characteristics and their impact on your life. In the Cosmic Glory Characteristics Domain of Existence, you discover who you are, how you live, and their implications regarding who you may become.

COSMIC GLORY
DRIVEN LIFE

In this cosmic model of human origin, life inexplicably comes from dead matter. This very act is a violation of its domain of inanimate material existence. In life, dead cosmic matter takes on what its domain of existence does not possess. Accordingly, all life on Earth came from the dead – dead matter. In this regard, its experience violates its existence. It may be that life and many of its characteristics indicate something beyond.

The question is: What kind of life does cosmic glory afford for its participants? Is this the kind of life you want to experience as your journey?

Remember, you can only experience what your chosen glory possesses. When your experience matches your chosen glory, you manifest personal integrity as to your chosen origin of being. To experience something contrary to its glory expressions is to embrace characteristics beyond its domain and imply origin beyond its essence. In life, it suggests an origin beyond the material sphere. When humans demonstrate characteristics beyond the cosmic order, they indicate origin beyond their domain of cosmic choice.

If you want a short trip in a universe of billions of years by age and perhaps hundreds of billions of light years in size, the comic journey may be your option. It's a short trip that maximizes feelings and minimizes meaning.

The glory-driven chart below is a chapter-by-chapter summary of this cosmic domain of existence. Every attempt has been made to provide a valid, appropriate, and reflective description of each glory-driven option. These profound ideas shape its glory-driven vision. Each chapter offers insights regarding one's Core of Being (COB) and Master of Ceremonies (MOC) projected into its future aspirations of potentiality.

In the model selected, what matters is not the question of certifying the validity of one's choice but the impact it brings to our lives. We are not trying to debate its merits (science versus religion) but to recognize its results. This approach allows us to envision the life we receive based on our selected origin. The origin becomes the domain of our existence and the source of life experiences. This domain thereby possesses the *totality* of all we can experience. Your origin or source equates to your life experience.

Please study "The Cosmic Glory Driven Model Characteristics" in chapter four of the SDL text to enhance your understanding of its description. The Cosmic Chart of Human Origin below will translate this description into a panoramic view of its implications for the human experience and journey.

COSMIC CHART OF HUMAN ORIGIN

The following characteristics, framing your identity, experiences, and vision, will guide and enable your life decisions, directions, and lifestyle choices. Follow your guides!

COSMIC DOMAIN OF EXISTENCE *FINITE INANIMATE MATERIAL DOMAIN – Matter and energy governed by physical laws – Cosmic Glory (C/G) – Why you exist / What you are.* ORIGIN DEFINES HUMAN CAPABILITIES From its material domain, humans discover what they are (DOE), why they exist (COG), who they are (COB), and how they live (MOC). It's a cosmic glory-driven intentional life strategy.			
C/G CORE OF BEING *Who you are* Identity	C/G MASTER OF CEREMONIES *How you live* MOCs Experience	C/G PROCESSES OF BECOMING *Processes for living* MOCs Applied	C/G PERSONAL VISION FORECAST *Whom you become* Aspirations
Elevate Your Potential - GBA			
Accidental Non-Special Unintentional Inanimate Material Being Chapter 1 *Earth Life* is an Informational DNA Being with a mind for rational capability, comprehension, and consciousness, demonstrating intentionality. Since these characteristics are not specific to the cosmic material domain, they may indicate another source of origin.	Strategic C/G MOC Characteristics for guidance and empowerment **Earth Life Intentionality** *– Accidental Inanimate Unintentional Atomic Matter – Mindless, Finite, Chance, randomness*	Your potential is dynamic as it merges aptitude, attitude, actions, and allocations! *Elevate your holistic potential through the "earth life mind" in its glory of intentionality with strategic planning and strategy.* Inexplicably, the cosmos gives us something (the universe) from nothing, "Earth Life" from dead matter, intentionality from unintentionality, and consciousness from unconsciousness. Question – How do earth life forms experience what the essential material universal domain does not possess?	In alignment with "Earth Life Glory (ELG)," *aspire to* **elevate your strategic potential with intentional initiatives** *(planning and strategy) in an unintentional cosmos.*

Cosmic Being of Phenomenal Potential Chapter 2	Performance C/G MOC Characteristics **Grow/increase/expand. Personal Growth** – *transcend self-constraints* and live beyond the limits of harmful feelings and conditions that discourage and defeat .	*Elevate your potential for growth/increase/expansion by transcending self-constraints in processes that master the art of stretching in the beyond arena – growing spiritually, personally, and professionally.*	Aspire to **Elevate your growth potential** by mastering the art of stretching in the beyond arena, transcending self-constraints – to become more than you can be .
Cosmic Being of Maturing Capability Chapter 3	Administrative C/G MOC Characteristics **Power-driven self-derived values** *for standards of maturing behavior – perhaps reflecting Fredrick Nietzsche's Übermensch or Superman*	*Elevate your potential for maturity by employing five keys to effective performance: authority specified, responsibility assumed, accountability applied, respect given, deficiency relieved, and strategy engaged—measured by performance standards of self-generated values.* The effectiveness of the standards constitutes the measure of maturity .	Aspire to **Elevate your maturing potential** with effective performance keys measured by self-generated values .
<td colspan="3">Design The Person You Want to Become</td>			
Cosmic Glory Being Chapter 4	Essential C/G MOC Characteristics **Cosmic Glory (DOE) Domain Characteristics** Finite demonstrations of *limitations in restrictions* Gravity as a force of *togetherness – attraction* Energy as a force of *separation – expansion* Entropy is a force that spreads out in *disorder – brokenness.* Terminations in final endings of absolute *death*	*Design the person you want to become in a Cosmic Glory short-term life.* Processes of finite limitations accent restrictions, gravity pulls with togetherness or attraction, and energy pushes apart in separations of expansion. At the same time, entropy spreads out in disordering brokenness, leading to terminations in eternal death.	*Out of your chosen C/G DOE Domain, aspire to* **design a cosmic glory short-term life** *of restrictions, togetherness, attractions, separations, brokenness, and eternal death.*

Cosmic Inspirational Being Chapter 5	Inspirational C/G MOC Characteristics **Universal Magnificence** amid Mysterious Majestic Beauty of Endless Symmetry in **Eternal Meaningless – Hopeless domain**	*Design an inspired inscribed heart with C/G characteristics for the person you want to become and the life you want to live.* Write in your heart magnificent inspirations of mysterious, majestic beauty punctuated with endless symmetry in motivating characteristics of hopeless cosmic glory-driven limitations.	*Out of your chosen C/G DOE Domain, Aspire to* **design an inscribed heart of characteristic hope-lessness** *in its magnifi-cent meaningless terminal universe.*
Cosmic Intelligent Being Chapter 6	Intelligence C/G MOC Characteristics **Material C/G Character Speaks Domain Rational** in spectacular Roaring Sounds of deficient Thought Cascading down the Hills of your Mind – Finite, closed-system limited potentially partial Intelligence. Scientists suggest that 5% of the universe is made of material atoms, comprising the totality of all we see and examine . This inference of partialness in both knowledge access and discernable capabilities is provocative .	*Design your intelligence as Cosmic Glory characteristics* displaying rational depictions of deficient limitations suggesting partialness as wholeness in processes like material experimentation, analysis, sequencing, vibrations, experiences, meditation, music, frequencies, and reflection for hearing sounds of limited cosmic material glory characteristics.	*Out of your chosen C/G DOE Domain, Aspire to* **design your partially in-formed mind** *(material only)* **as intellectual whole-ness** *in deficient sounds of universal limitations.*

Define The Spirituality That Defines You			
Cosmic Spiritual Being Chapter 7	<u>Meaningful</u> C/G MOC Characteristics *Material All-natural Physical* **Experiential Spirituality** *"A cosmic religion... it should arise from the experience of all things, natural and spiritual, as a meaningful unity." Albert Einstei*n	*Define a C/G spirituality of natural and physical experience that is meaningful and unifying. There are three basic types of spirituality: individualism, collectivism, and dialogue. Individualism espouses personal identity, development, and meaning. It's up to the individual to embrace the totality of life as they see it. Collectivism, in spirituality, is the unifying domain of religion. It is often highly relational and configured by divine wisdom. Dialogue spirituality engenders change and growth through deep listening, empathy, and openness with transparency. In dialogue, the wisdom of the ages is sought through the shared ideas of ancient and modern human understanding. In each type of spirituality—existence, expression, and experience must be aligned, as you can only experience what your domain of origin possesses.*	*Aspire to define a **C/G experiential spirituality** expressed in its natural and physical domains that is meaningful and unifying.*
Cosmic Set-apart Being Chapter 8	<u>Set-apart</u> C/G MOC Characteristics **Set-apart or premier All-natural physical, spiritual experiences** – *in material or human manifestation*s "As the sacred goes, so goes the world" SDL text .	*Define your C/G natural or physical spirituality in premier or set-apart expressions of material or human forms (the sacred) in processes* like rituals, celebrations, and pilgrimages for an all-natural spirituality of set-apart images and behaviors from which laws forcibly and universally shape the future.	*Aspire to **define the most meaningful C/G experiential spirituality** in set-apart material or human manifestations.*
Cosmic Relational Being Chapter 9	<u>Relational</u> C/G MOC Characteristics **Anti-Relational Self-Interest Relationships**	*Define your relational spirituality in C/G self-interest behaviors through processes of short-term self-interest associations – brokenness.*	*Aspire to **define C/G spirituality in human relationships** as short-term self-interest human associations of brokenness.*

Cosmic Community Being Chapter 10	Community C/G MOC Characteristics **Dynamic Material Partnerships**	*Define your community spirituality in material-driven partnerships,* generating a material lifestyle without a basis for fulfillment, ethics, morality, and equality, fostering resentment and hate .	*Aspire to* **define a C/G material spirituality** *as a community culture of material-driven partnerships.*
Cosmic Source-defined Being Chapter 11	Source C/G MOC Characteristics **A C/G Material source, self-defined being.**	*Define your being/identity in a C/G material source, generating a material culture of experiential spirituality so that self-determinations become absolute (without transcendent ethics) in a community of increasing and unrestricted corruption.*	Aspire to **define a C/G human spirituality** *as a human-derived, human-defined, short-term experiential humanity.*

▶ *ACTION ITEM SEVEN: Specify meaningful observations about the Cosmic Human Origin Chart. To increase comprehension, share these beneficial observations with others in your Discovery Group.*

On pages 26 - 36, you will discover the Empowerment of MOC Glory Characteristics – Be Glory Empowered in a Glory-filled Life.

COSMIC GLORY DRIVEN LIFE
MASTER OF CEREMONIES (MOC) STRATEGY

As illustrated in this workbook, develop your MOC Cosmic Glory Driven Life Strategy for each module . Feel free to adjust the MOCs as you feel appropriate . This exercise aims to recognize the MOC influence gained from each model of human origin as applied to the life of each of its adherents .

- Elevate Your Potential – C/G MOC Strategy
  - ▶ *ACTION ITEM* – C/G Progress Potential
- Design The Person You Want to Become – MOC Strategy
  - ▶ *ACTION ITEM* – C/G Becoming Potential
- Define The Spirituality That Defines You – MOC Strategy
  - ▶ *ACTION ITEM* – C/G Spiritual Potential

Selecting a cosmic human origin can help you discover the glorious characteristics that define the person you want to become and the kind of life you want to experience according to the material domain. In cosmic origin, you will align your Center of Gravity (COG), Core of Being (COB), and Master of Ceremonies (MOC) with your identity and experience in your cosmic world.

In your selection of the cosmic origin, MOCs are limited to the glory of the cosmos. As you implement these MOCs into your life, you become their glory in your person and world – a living discipleship of your origin of choice, a cosmic material being.

MOCs are expressions of your COG domain and possess the powers of your origin. In the cosmic origin, they are limited and temporal as defined by their domain of existence. They represent the power of the universe, expressed as the glory characteristic that origin possesses. Therefore, they shape your life and journey with an impact that transforms you into their likeness. They become your potential in the material world.

There is a three-step process for implementing your selected MOCs into your life experience. *Value* their domain significance – adoration/worship. *Live* their influential capabilities – lifestyle/discipleship. *Become* the characteristics of their essence – likeness, an incarnational effect. MOCs are continuously inscribed (written) in your heart in this process of value, lifestyle, and becoming. Embrace your selected MOCs in this three-step process.

COSMIC CHART OF HUMAN ORIGIN

Elevate Your Potential – GBA			
Accidental Non-Special Unintentional Inanimate Material Being Chapter 1 *Earth Life* is an Informational DNA Being with a mind for rational capability, comprehension, and consciousness, demonstrating intentionality. Since these characteristics are not specific to the cosmic material domain, they may indicate another source of origin.	Strategic C/G MOC Characteristics for guidance and empowerment **Earth Life Intentionality** *– Accidental Inanimate Unintentional Atomic Matter – Mindless, Finite, Chance, randomness*	Your potential is dynamic as it merges aptitude, attitude, actions, and assignments! *Elevate your holistic potential through the "earth life mind" in its glory of intentionality with strategic planning and strategy.* Inexplicably, the cosmos gives us something (the universe) from nothing, "Earth Life" from dead matter, intentionality from unintentionality, and consciousness from unconsciousness. <u>Question</u> – How do earth life forms experience what the essential material universal domain does not possess?	In alignment with "Earth Life Glory (ELG)," *aspire to* **elevate your strategic potential with intentional initiatives** *(planning and strategy) in an unintentional cosmos.*
Cosmic Being of Phenomenal Potential Chapter 2	Performance C/G MOC Characteristics **Grow/increase/expand. Personal Growth** *– transcend self-constraints* and live beyond the limits of harmful feelings and conditions that discourage and defeat.	*Elevate your potential for growth/increase/expansion by transcending self-constraints in processes that master the art of stretching in the beyond arena – growing spiritually, personally, and professionally.*	Aspire to **Elevate your growth potential** *by mastering the art of stretching in the beyond arena, transcending self-constraints* – to become more than you can be.
Cosmic Being of Maturing Capability Chapter 3	Administrative C/G MOC Characteristics **Power-driven self-derived values** *for standards of maturing behavior – perhaps reflecting Fredrick Nietzsche's Übermensch or Superman*	*Elevate your potential for maturity by employing five keys to effective performance: authority specified, responsibility assumed, accountability applied, respect given, deficiency relieved, and strategy engaged—measured by performance standards of self-generated values.* The effectiveness of the standards constitutes the measure of maturity.	Aspire to **Elevate your maturing potential** with effective performance keys measured by self-generated values.

Module One: ELEVATE YOUR POTENTIAL – Through implementing your Cosmic Glory MOC characteristics.

You will Elevate Your Potential by employing the Cosmic Glory (C/G) MOC characteristics below. In the process of adoration, lifestyle, and likeness, MOCs are written in your heart. What you write in your heart determines who you become and the life you experience. "For as he thinketh in his heart, so is he" (Proverbs 23:7). This inscribed MOC heart shapes you by inserting its likeness, knowledge, and transforming influence. *Follow inscribed MOCs to be Glory-Empowered!*

Please note that the MOCs inscribed in the heart bring to their recipient the presence of its MOC reality, the knowledge that the MOC reality possesses, and the transforming effect that the MOC reality provides. *This MOC presence, knowledge, and transforming effect is glory empowerment!*

Employ the C/G MOC glory characteristics for elevating your potential:

Chapter One – Strategic C/G – ELG Characteristics – Cosmic Glory (C/G) – accidental inanimate material cosmos – Earth-Life Glory (ELG) – intentionally

> *Value – C/G Randomness – Adore*
>
> *Live – Randomly – Lifestyle*
>
> *Be – Random – Likeness*
>
> *Value – ELG Intentionality – Adore*
>
> *Live – Intentionally – Lifestyle*
>
> *Be – Intentional – Likeness – plan and strategy*

Chapter Two – Performance C/G – ELG Characteristics – Earth-life Growth

> *Value – ELG Growth – Adore*
>
> *Live – Growingly – Lifestyle*
>
> *Be – Growing – Likeness – a growth-oriented person*

Chapter Three – Administrative C/G – ELG Characteristics – Earth-life Subjective values – C/G Power-driven life (support values)

> *Value – C/G Power-driven life – Adore*
>
> *Live – Power-driven – Lifestyle*
>
> *Be – Power – Likeness – become powerful*
>
> *Value – ELG Subjectivity – Adore*
>
> *Live – Subjectively – Lifestyle*
>
> *Be – Subjective (power-driven values) – Likeness*

> ▶ *ACTION ITEM EIGHT: C/G Elevating Potential – Inscribe the above* <u>*Life-Elevating*</u> *C/G MOC characteristics in your heart. MOCs are written in your heart through adoration, lifestyle, and likeness, bringing presence, knowledge, and transforming influence – Cosmic Glory Likeness. Share with your Discovery Group at least one elevating impact these MOCs have on your life.*

Design The Person You Want to Become – Master of Ceremonies Strategy

<table>
<tr><th colspan="4">Design The Person You Want to Become</th></tr>
<tr>
<td>Cosmic Glory Being Chapter 4</td>
<td>Essential C/G
MOC Characteristics

Cosmic Glory (DOE) Domain Characteristics

<u>Finite</u> demonstrations of *limitations in restrictions*
<u>Gravity</u> as a force of *togetherness – attraction*
<u>Energy</u> as a force of *separation – expansion*
<u>Entropy</u> is a force that spreads out in *disorder –brokenness.*
<u>Terminations</u> in final endings of absolute *death*</td>
<td>*Design the person you want to become in a Cosmic Glory short-term life.* Processes of finite limitations accent restrictions, gravity pulls with togetherness or attraction, and energy pushes apart in separations of expansion. At the same time, entropy spreads out in disordering brokenness, leading to terminations in eternal death.</td>
<td>*Out of your chosen C/G DOE Domain, aspire to* ***design a cosmic glory short-term life*** *of restrictions, togetherness, attractions, separations, brokenness, and eternal death.*</td>
</tr>
<tr>
<td>Cosmic Inspirational Being Chapter 5</td>
<td><u>Inspirational</u> C/G
MOC Characteristics

Universal Magnificence *amid Mysterious Majestic Beauty of Endless Symmetry in* ***Eternal Meaningless – Hopeless domain***</td>
<td>*Design an inspired inscribed heart with C/G characteristics for the person you want to become and the life you want to live.* Write in your heart magnificent inspirations of mysterious, majestic beauty punctuated with endless symmetry in motivating characteristics of hopeless cosmic glory-driven limitations.</td>
<td>*Out of your chosen C/G DOE Domain, Aspire to* ***design an inscribed heart of characteristic hopelessness*** *in its magnificent meaningless terminal universe.*</td>
</tr>
</table>

Cosmic Intelligent Being Chapter 6	Intelligence C/G MOC Characteristics ***Material C/G Character Speaks Domain Rational*** *in spectacular Roaring Sounds of deficient Thought Cascading down the Hills of your Mind* – Finite, closed-system limited potentially partial Intelligence. Scientists suggest that 5% of the universe is made of material atoms, comprising the totality of all we see and examine. This inference of partialness in both knowledge access and discernable capabilities is provocative.	*Design your intelligence as Cosmic Glory characteristics* displaying rational depictions of deficient limitations suggesting partialness as wholeness in processes like material experimentation, analysis, sequencing, vibrations, experiences, meditation, music, frequencies, and reflection for hearing sounds of limited cosmic material glory characteristics.	*Out of your chosen C/G DOE Domain, Aspire to* ***design your partially informed mind as intellectual wholeness*** *in deficient sounds of universal limitations.*

Module Two: DESIGN THE PERSON YOU WANT TO BECOME – Through implementing your chosen C/G MOCs.

You will design the person you want to become as you employ the Cosmic Glory (C/G) MOC characteristics below. In the processes of adoration/worship, lifestyle/discipleship, and likeness, MOCs are inscribed in your heart. What you write in your heart determines who you become and the life you experience. "For as he thinketh in his heart, so is he" (Proverbs 23:7). This inscribed heart of MOC glory shapes you by sharing its likeness, knowledge, and transforming influence. *Follow inscribed MOCs to be Glory-Empowered!*

Please note that the MOCs inscribed in the heart bring to their recipient the presence of its MOC reality, the knowledge that the MOC reality possesses, and the transforming effect that the MOC reality provides. *This MOC presence, knowledge, and transforming effect is glory empowerment!*

Employ the C/G MOC glory characteristics for designing the person you want to become:

<u>Chapter Four – C/G Characteristics</u> – Cosmic Glory-driven Short-term Experience – limited/ restricted, expansion/separation, togetherness/attraction, brokenness/death. C/G destiny of death. Select from these MOC elements or others you feel appropriate.

      Value – C/G Magnificent Short-term Life – Adore

      Live – Short-term Magnificence – Lifestyle

      Be – A Magnificent Short-term Life – Likeness

<u>Chapter Five – Inspiring C/G Characteristics</u> – Eternal Hopelessness in a Magnificent Universe

      Value – C/G Eternal Hopelessness – Adore

      Live – Hopelessly – Lifestyle

Be – Hopeless – Likeness

Chapter Six – Intelligent C/G Characteristics – Thoughts of Cosmic Glory Characteristics

Value – C/G Material-aligned Holistic-Assumed Thoughts – Adore

Live – Material-aligned Holistic-Assumed Reasoning – Lifestyle

Be – Material-aligned Holistic-Assumed Intelligence – Likeness

---

▶ *ACTION ITEM NINE: C/G Designing Possibilities – Inscribe the above* <u>*Life-Shaping*</u> *C/G MOC characteristics in your heart. MOCs are written in your heart through adoration, lifestyle, and likeness, bringing presence, knowledge, and transforming influence – Cosmic Glory Likeness. Share with your Discovery Group at least one personal design impact these MOCs have on your life.*

Define The Spirituality That Defines You			
Cosmic Spiritual Being Chapter 7	<u>Meaningful</u> C/G MOC Characteristics *Material All-natural Physical* **Experiential Spirituality** *"A cosmic religion… it should arise from the experience of all things, natural and spiritual, as a meaningful unity." Albert Einstein*	*Define a C/G spirituality of natural and physical experience that is meaningful and unifying. There are three basic types of spirituality: individualism, collectivism, and dialogue. Individualism espouses personal identity, development, and meaning. It's up to the individual to embrace the totality of life as they see it. Collectivism, in spirituality, is the unifying domain of religion. It is often highly relational and configured by divine wisdom. Dialogue spirituality engenders change and growth through deep listening, empathy, and openness with transparency. In dialogue, the wisdom of the ages is sought through the shared ideas of ancient and modern human understanding. In each type of spirituality—existence, expression, and experience must be aligned, as you can only experience what your domain of origin possesses.*	*Aspire to define a* **C/G experiential spirituality** *expressed in its natural and physical domains that is meaningful and unifying.*
Cosmic Set-apart Being Chapter 8	<u>Set-apart</u> C/G MOC Characteristics **Set-apart or premier All-natural physical, spiritual experiences – in** *material or human manifestations* "As the sacred goes, so goes the world" SDL text.	*Define your C/G natural or physical spirituality in premier or set-apart expressions of material or human forms (the sacred) in processes* like rituals, celebrations, and pilgrimages for an all-natural spirituality of set-apart images and behaviors from which laws forcibly and universally shape the future.	*Aspire to* **define the most meaningful C/G experiential spirituality** *in set-apart material or human manifestations.*
Cosmic Relational Being Chapter 9	<u>Relational</u> C/G MOC Characteristics **Anti-Relational Self-Interest Relationships**	*Define your relational spirituality in C/G self-interest behaviors* through processes of short-term self-interest associations – brokenness.	*Aspire to* **define C/G spirituality in human relationships** *as short-term self-interest human associations of brokenness.*

Cosmic Community Being Chapter 10	<u>Community</u> C/G MOC Characteristics ***Dynamic Material Partnerships***	*Define your community spirituality in material-driven partnerships,* generating a material lifestyle without a basis for fulfillment, ethics, morality, and equality, fostering resentment and hate .￼	*Aspire to **define a C/G material spirituality** as a community culture of material-driven partnerships.*
Cosmic Source-defined Being Chapter 11	<u>Source</u> C/G MOC Characteristics ***A C/G Material source, self-defined being.***	*Define your being/identity in a C/G material source, generating a material culture of experiential spirituality so that self-determinations become absolute (without transcendent ethics) in a community of increasing and unrestricted corruption.*	Aspire to ***define a C/G human spirituality*** *as a human-derived, human-defined, short-term experiential humanity.*

Module Three: DEFINE THE SPIRITUALITY THAT DEFINES YOU – Through Implementing your chosen C/G MOCs .

As you employ the below Cosmic Glory (C/G) MOC characteristics that define your spirituality, that spirituality will define you. In the processes of adoration/worship, lifestyle/discipleship, and likeness, MOCs are inscribed in your heart. What you write in your heart determines who you become and the life you experience. "For as he thinketh in his heart, so is he" (Proverbs 23:7). This inscribed MOC characteristic heart shapes you by sharing its glory, likeness, knowledge, and transforming influence. Follow inscribed MOCs to be Glory-Empowered!

Please note that the MOCs inscribed in the heart bring to their recipient the presence of its MOC reality, the knowledge that the MOC reality possesses, and the transforming effect that the MOC reality provides. *This MOC presence, knowledge, and transforming effect is glory empowerment!*

C/G MOC glory characteristics for defining the spirituality that defines you:

Chapter Seven – C/G Experiential Spiritual Characteristics – Experiencing the material, physical, and natural world.

> Value – Meaningful Experiences – Adore
>
> Live – Experiences of Meaning – Lifestyle
>
> Be – Experiential Meanings – Likeness

Chapter Eight – Set-apart Characteristics – All-natural spiritual experiences in set-apart material/physical forms

> Value – Most Meaningful (set apart) Experiences – Adore
>
> Live – Most Popular (set apart) experiences – Lifestyle
>
> Be – Set Apart (sacred) Experiences – likeness

Chapter Nine – C/G Relational Characteristics – Anti-relational self-interest spirituality

> Value – Self-interest, Short-term Relationships – Adore
>
> Live – Self-interest Relationships – Lifestyle
>
> Be – Short-term Relationships – Likeness

Chapter Ten – Community Characteristics – A material-driven partnership community

> Value – Material Partnerships – Adore
>
> Live – Material Associations – Lifestyle
>
> Be – A Material Partner – Likeness.

Chapter Eleven – Source Characteristics – A material (source-defined) being

> Value – A Material Source – Adore
>
> Live – Materially – Lifestyle
>
> Be – Material (source-derived being) – likeness

> ▶ *ACTION ITEM TEN: C/G Defining Spirituality – Inscribe the above <u>Life-Enriching</u> C/G MOC characteristics in your heart. MOCs are written in your heart through adoration, lifestyle, and likeness, bringing presence, knowledge, and transforming influence – Cosmic Glory Likeness. Share with your Discovery Group at least one spiritual impact these MOCs have on your life.*

Now, you are ready to build your Cosmic Glory-Driven SDL Vision as presented in pages 37- 49. In this visionary strategy, you will merge a glory-driven strategic *plan* with a glory-driven strategic *strategy*, shaping your future *aspirations* accomplished through SMART *goals* for achieving your *visionary design*.

COSMIC GLORY-DRIVEN MASTER OF CEREMONIES
A Cosmic Character-Driven Life

▶ Be Intentional / Randomness – Cosmic Glory

▶ Be Intentional / Intentionality – Earth Life Cosmic Glory

▶ Be More / Growing Potential – Beyond (Transcend) Self Constraints

▶ Be Distinguished / Maturing Potential – Subjective Power-driven Values

▶ Be Discerning / Cosmic Glory-driven Life – Short-Term Living

▶ Be Inspired / Cosmic Glory-driven Heart – Inscribed Hopelessness

▶ Be Intelligent / Cosmic Glory-driven Mind – Material-Aligned (Holistic-Assumed) Intelligence – C/G Limited Illusionary Partialness

▶ Be Spiritual / All-Natural Experiential Spirituality – Meaning

▶ Be Greatness / Set Apart (sacred) – Most Meaningful Experiences

▶ Be Holy / Self-interest Associations – Broken Relationships

▶ Be Unmeasurable / Material Associations – Fulfillment

▶ Be Legacy / Material Being – Brokenness in Everlasting Death

If you wish to employ other cosmic characteristics as your MOC, please feel free to use its guidance in your life. For validity, ensure that it exists in your chosen domain of origin. You can only experience what your domain of origin possesses.

COSMIC GLORY DRIVEN LIFE
VISIONARY STRATEGY

Cosmic glory is determinative regarding one's future potential . The only vision you can embrace is the one cosmic glory provides . This exercise helps you to see the future cosmic glory envisions . The related goals and steps for accomplishments are personal to you and applied at your discretion .

C/G Visionary Life Strategy

- Elevate Your Potential – C/G Potential Visionary Strategy
  - ▶ ACTION ITEM – C/G Vision of Potential
- Design the Person You Want to Become – C/G Personal Visionary Strategy
  - ▶ ACTION ITEM – C/G Vision of Personal Growth
- Define The Spirituality That Defines You – C/G Spiritual Visionary Strategy
  - ▶ ACTION ITEM – C/G Vision of Spiritual Life

Each chapter will give three components that shape your life and vision.

- Your C/G – MOC for guidance and empowerment
- Your C/G – Strategic Plan in your Behavioral Objective
- Your C/G – Strategic Strategy of Intentionality – defined in your aspirations, as noted in your Human Origin Charts

Elevate Your Potential – C/G Potential SDL Visionary GDL Strategy

<u>Chapter One</u>:

C/G MOC – Be Intentional – Earth Life / Cosmic Glory Strategy

Processes for being intentional – plan and strategy.

> *Behavioral Objective –* **Strategic Plan**
>
> > Build your SDL vision as an intentional, empowered, Earth Life Cosmic GDL strategy
>
> *Aspiration –* Intentional Strategic Strategy
>
> > Elevate your strategic potential with intentional Earth Life Cosmic Glory-driven strategies or initiatives in an unintentional random-driven universe.
>
> *Life Empowerment –* for strategic achievements.
>
> > Celebrate Calculated Achievements!

Set your goals for elevating your *strategic potential* with *intentionality as an SDL Earth Life Cosmic random glory-driven strategy.* Gain insight from chapter one in the Cosmic Chart of Human Origin.

SMART Goal 1 –

_____

Specify steps to accomplish your goal.

1. _____

2. _____

3. _____

Celebrate each step's achievement!

    Record in your journal – How, with whom, and where.

SMART Goal 2.

_____

Specify steps to accomplish your goal.

1. _____

2. _____

3. _____

Celebrate each step's achievement!

Record in your journal – How, with whom, and where.

Employ more goals if needed.

In your journal, record your progress. Then celebrate!

<u>Chapter Two:</u>

C/G MOC – Be More - Become Growing Potential

Processes for Growing!

    Behavioral Objective – Strategic Plan

        Become more than you can be

    Aspiration – Strategic Strategy

        Master the art of stretching

    Life empowerment – for strategic accomplishments.

        Stretch in the Beyond Arena

        Celebrate calculated achievements!

Set your goals for elevating your *growth beyond self-constraints* by *mastering the art of stretching in the beyond arena.* Gain insight from chapter two in the Cosmic Chart of Human Origin.

SMART Goal 1 –

_____

Specify steps to accomplish your goal.

1. _____

2. _____

3. _____

Celebrate each step's achievement!

    Record in your journal – How, with whom, and where.

SMART Goal 2.

_____

Specify steps to accomplish your goal.

1. _____

2. _____

3. _____

Celebrate each step's achievement!

    Record in your journal – How, with whom, and where.

Employ more goals if needed.

In your journal, record your progress. Then celebrate!

Chapter Three:

C/G MOC – Be Distinguished – Assume Responsibility for Subjective Power-driven values

Potential Processes of Maturity!

    Behavioral Objective – Strategic Plan

        Become a person of maturing distinction in C/G subjective value-derived standards

    Aspiration – Strategic Strategy

        Employ subjective value-derived standards in all Five Leadership Keys for maturing potential.

    Life empowerment – for strategic accomplishments

        Assume responsibility for life and mission.

        Celebrate calculated achievements!

Set specific goals for elevating your maturing potential by employing life actions in subjective value-derived standards. Gain insight from chapter three in the Cosmic Chart of Human Origin.

SMART Goal 1 –

_____

Specify steps to accomplish your goal.

1. _____

2. _____

3. _____

Celebrate each step's achievement!

    Record in your journal – How, with whom, and where.

SMART Goal 2.

_____

Specify steps to accomplish your goal.

1. _____

2. _____

3. _____

Celebrate each step's achievement!

    Record in your journal – How, with whom, and where.

Employ more goals if needed.

    In your journal, record your progress. Then celebrate!

▶ *ACTION ITEM ELEVEN: Accomplish your above Visionary Performance Goals for Elevating Your C/G-driven Potential by achieving the steps you have set for their fulfillment. Celebrate your achievements with those who share your life's journey. Describe your celebration event and those who celebrated with you. Record specific actions you or others performed to commemorate your accomplishments.*

Chapter Four:

C/G MOC – Be Discerning – Become a Cosmic Glory-Driven life of Short-term Living

Processes for C/G MOC engagement!

>   *Behavioral Objective* – Strategic Plan

>> Become a person of value with meaning and purpose – Significance!

>   *Aspiration* – Strategic Strategy

>> Design a cosmic glory short-term magnificent life of endless restrictions.

>   *Life empowerment* – for strategic accomplishments.

>> The power of choice

>> Celebrate calculated achievements!

Set goals for designing the *C/G short-term life characteristic person* you want to become *using processes of finite limitations.* Gain insight from chapter four in the Cosmic Chart of Human Origin.

SMART Goal 1 –

_____

Specify steps to accomplish your goal.

1. _____

2. _____

3. _____

Celebrate each step's achievement!

>   Record in your journal – How, with whom, and where.

SMART Goal 2.

_____

Specify steps to accomplish your goal.

1. _____

2. _____

3. _____

Celebrate each step's achievement!

>   Record in your journal – How, with whom, and where.

Employ more goals if needed.

>   In your journal, record your progress. Then celebrate!

Chapter Five:

C/G MOC – Be Inspired – Inscribed Hopelessness

Processes for inscribed heart inspirations!

> *Behavioral Objective –* **Strategic Plan**
>
>> Inscribe, write in your heart, your chosen glory characteristics as the core of who you are.
>
> *Aspiration –* **Strategic Strategy**
>
>> Design an inscribed heart of characteristic magnificence wrapped in a hopeless terminal universe. You can only experience what your domain of existence possesses.
>
> *Life empowerment –* for strategic accomplishments.
>
>> Passion from an inscribed heart
>>
>> Celebrate calculated achievements!

Set goals for designing the *C/G heart of magnificent characteristics wrapped in a hopeless terminal universe manifesting processes awaiting eternal endings.* Gain insight from chapter five in the Cosmic Chart of Human Origin.

SMART Goal 1 –

_____

Specify steps to accomplish your goal.

1. _____

2. _____

3. _____

Celebrate each step's achievement!

> Record in your journal – How, with whom, and where.

SMART Goal 2.

_____

Specify steps to accomplish your goal.

1. _____

2. _____

3. _____

Celebrate each step's achievement!

> Record in your journal – How, with whom, and where.

Employ more goals if needed;

> In your journal, record your progress. Then celebrate!

Chapter Six:

C/G MOC – Be Intelligent – C/G Limited Partial Closed System Intelligence

Processes for a C/G Intelligence!

Behavioral Objective – Strategic Plan

Design your mind (hear, learn, think) as the material-aligned (holistically assumed) closed intelligence your cosmic glory possesses – limited partial closed system intelligence.

Aspiration – Intelligence – Strategic Strategy

Hear the spectacular sounds of "Cosmic Glory Characteristics" roaring with deficient thoughts in a partially informed intelligence – depictions of limited/partial, closed system glory.

Life empowerment – for strategic accomplishments.

Listen to the music

Celebrate calculated achievements!

Set goals for designing the *material-aligned, holistically assumed mind, of a closed system sounds of partial intelligence in processes of limited (5%?) partiality.* Gain insight from chapter six in the Cosmic Chart of Human Origin.

SMART Goal 1 –

_____

Specify steps to accomplish your goal.

1. _____

2. _____

3. _____

Celebrate each step's achievement!

Record in your journal – How, with whom, and where.

SMART Goal 2.

_____

Specify steps to accomplish your goal.

1. _____

2. _____

3. _____

Celebrate each step's achievement!

Record in your journal – How, with whom, and where.

Employ more goals if needed. Then Celebrate!

> ▶ *ACTION ITEM TWELVE: Accomplish your above Visionary Personal Design Goals for Becoming The C/G-driven Person You Want to Become by achieving the steps you have set for their fulfillment. Celebrate your achievements with those who share your life's journey. Describe your celebration event and those who celebrated with you. Record specific actions you or others performed to commemorate your accomplishments.*

DEFINE THE SPIRITUALITY THAT DEFINES YOU – *C/G Spiritual SDL Visionary GDL Strategy*

Chapter Seven:

C/G MOC – Be Spiritual - Become C/G All-Natural Experiential Spirituality

Processes for experiencing the all-natural world!

> *Behavioral Objective –* **Strategic Plan**

>> Become the Cosmic Glory-Driven experiential spirituality that defines you

> Aspiration – Experience Spirituality as a Strategic Strategy

>> Employ a C/G all-natural (material and physical) experiential spirituality for all humanity

> Life empowerment – for strategic accomplishments.

>> Wind beneath your wings

>> Celebrate calculated achievements!

Set goals for defining the *all-natural physical experiential spirituality* that defines you – *experiences that aim to bring meaning and unity.* Gain insight from chapter seven in the Cosmic Chart of Human Origin.

SMART Goal 1 –

_____

Specify steps to accomplish your goal.

1. _____

2. _____

3. _____

Celebrate each step's achievement!

> Record in your journal – How, with whom, and where.

SMART Goal 2.

_____

Specify steps to accomplish your goal.

1. _____

2. _____

3. _____

Celebrate each step's achievement!

    Record in your journal – How, with whom, and where.

Employ more goals if needed.

    In your journal, record your progress. Then celebrate!

Chapter Eight:

C/G MOC – Be Greatness - Become Set-Apart Experiential Spirituality.

Processes for set-apart material and physical manifestations of all-natural experiences!

    Behavioral Objective – Strategic Plan

        Give your world a great future – your strategic imperative of sacred value

    Aspiration – Strategic Strategy

        Value set apart (most significant) or sacred material and physical manifestations of all-natural experiential spirituality

    Life empowerment – for strategic accomplishments.

        Value the sacred – set apart.

        Celebrate calculated achievements!

Set goals for defining the _most significant experiential spirituality_ that defines you – _valuing set-apart material and physical all-natural experiences._ Gain insight from chapter eight in the Cosmic Chart of Human Origin.

SMART Goal 1 –

_____

Specify steps to accomplish your goal.

1. _____

2. _____

3. _____

Celebrate each step's achievement!

    Record in your journal – How, with whom, and where.

SMART Goal 2.

_____

Specify steps to accomplish your goal.

1. _____

2. _____

3. _____

Celebrate each step's achievement!

Record in your journal – How, with whom, and where.

Employ more goals if needed.

In your journal, record your progress. Then celebrate!

Chapter Nine:

C/G MOC – Be Holy – Become wholistic Relational Spirituality.

Processes for self-interest experiential relationships of brokenness!

Behavioral Objective – Strategic Plan

Become Cosmic Glory-Driven experiential, short-term relationships of brokenness

Aspiration – Strategic Strategy

Create wholeness in short-term self-interest associations as broken relationships of C/G experiential spirituality.

Life empowerment – for strategic accomplishments.

The power of one

Celebrate calculated achievements!

Goals for defining the _self-interest experiential spirituality_ that defines you – _short-term self-interest broken relationships._ Gain insight from chapter nine in the Cosmic Chart of Human Origin.

SMART Goal 1 –

_____

Specify steps to accomplish your goal.

1. _____

2. _____

3. _____

Celebrate each step's achievement!

Record in your journal – How, with whom, and where.

SMART Goal 2.

_____

Specify steps to accomplish your goal.

1. _____

2. _____

3. _____

Celebrate each step's achievement!

  Record in your journal – How, with whom, and where.

Employ more goals if needed.

  In your journal, record your progress. Then celebrate!

Chapter Ten:

C/G MOC – Be Unmeasurable – Become Partners in a Cultural Experiential Spirituality.

Processes for building material partnerships!

  Behavioral Objective – Strategic Plan

    Build a Beyond Culture of C/G material-driven partnerships.

  Aspiration – Strategic Strategy

    Produce a community of material-driven partnerships in self-interest relationships.

  Life empowerment – for strategic accomplishments.

    Exponential power levels

    Celebrate calculated achievements!

Goals for defining the *experiential cultural spirituality* that defines you – *build material-driven partnerships in self-interest relationships.* Gain insight from chapter ten in the Cosmic Chart of Human Origin.

SMART Goal 1 –

_____

Specify steps to accomplish your goal.

1. _____

2. _____

3. _____

Celebrate each step's achievement!

  Record in your journal – How, with whom, and where.

SMART Goal 2.

_____

Specify steps to accomplish your goal.

1. _____

2. _____

3. _____

Celebrate each step's achievement!

    Record in your journal – How, with whom, and where.

Employ more goals if needed.

    In your journal, record your progress. Then celebrate!

Chapter Eleven:

C/G MOC – Be Legacy - Become Source-driven Experiential Spirituality.

Processes for a Source-driven human being!

    Behavioral Objective – Source-defined Strategic Plan

        Maximize C/G Source-driven stewardship that matures Source-defined influence.

    Aspiration – Strategic Strategy

        Embrace the seven processes of C/G Source-defined beneficial influence.

    Life empowerment – for strategic accomplishments.

        The power in your serve

        Celebrate calculated achievements!

Set goals for defining the *Source-defined spirituality* that defines you – *become a C/G Source-driven Source-defined being.* Gain insight from chapter eleven in the Cosmic Chart of Human Origin.

SMART Goal 1 –

_____

Specify steps to accomplish your goal.

1. _____

2. _____

3. _____

Celebrate each step's achievement!

    Record in your journal – How, with whom, and where.

SMART Goal 2.

_____

Specify steps to accomplish your goal.

1. _____

2. _____

3. _____

Celebrate each step's achievement!

    Record in your journal – How, with whom, and where.

Employ more goals if needed.

    In your journal, record your progress. Then celebrate!

> ▶ *ACTION ITEM THIRTEEN: Accomplish your above Spiritual Goals for Your C/G-driven Visionary Spirituality by achieving the steps you have set for their fulfillment. Celebrate your achievements with those who share your life's journey. Describe your celebration event and those who celebrated with you. Record specific actions you or others performed to commemorate your accomplishments.*

Congratulations!

You Have Completed Your Cosmic Glory-Driven SDL Vision!

Your vision is specified in your goals and steps of achievement. With the empowerment of your MOCs and the projection of your aspirations for life, you are well-suited to engage your future with confidence and commitment. Keep your journal active, recording significant accomplishments that demonstrate your journey in your newly acquired capabilities of vision and MOC energies. It is your life envisioned and empowered to perform.

Let's proceed with the Creator/cosmic glory-driven SDL vision.

CREATOR COSMIC (C/c) GLORY-DRIVEN LIFE

The second human origin option is the Creator/cosmic (C/c) glory-driven model . In your selection of this model, MOCs express the glory of the Creator and cosmos . As you implement these MOCs into your life, you become their glory in your person and world – a living discipleship of your origin of choice, a Creator/ cosmic Spirit/material being .

The combined Creator/cosmic-driven glory model provides the best of both worlds. It maximizes benefits and minimizes deficiencies. It is a visionary future with the extraordinary potential of hope beyond all terminations. It's your choice in everlasting life.

The C/c MOCs reflect the character of the Creator and His essence of everlasting life. Consider four MOC glory characteristics that guided and empowered Jesus' journey – the Sacred, Holy Wholeness (oneness with the Father and Holy Spirit), Truth in the Words of Life, and the Will of God. Jesus gained victory over Lucifer through the sacred. The sacred is the material manifestation of the holy. And since calvary humans as the temple of God manifest the holiness of God in the flesh as Christ's reflection. The holy always defeats evil and its strategies of iniquity—adherence to the sacred stops in its track's wickedness in high places.

The intentional Will of God MOC took Christ to the cross and brought Him out of the grave. Even when you are seemingly dead or incapacitated in the trials of life, the MOC will of God prevails. When the final epitaph has been written, the MOC of everlasting life in the will of God rises above with ultimate victory over that which seeks its demise. The stone always moves at the will of God, while the grave gives up what it could not hold. Victory is a core domain of C/c MOC characterizations. The more MOCs you embrace, inscribed in your heart, the more the Creator's character abides in you and the more of His victory you experience.

In worship and discipleship, MOCs live in you, granting you the capabilities of who they are. Embrace them with the wonder of magic in the miracle. Live with anticipation as they bring more than you can imagine to your journey. In C/c glory MOCs, you will discover God's manifest presence that will never leave you—granting God's elevating revelations of truth and powers of personal and corporate transformation. As Moses' life illustrates, the abiding presence of the glory of the Creator/cosmos suggests the ordinary should be concerned (look out), for the extraordinary may become commonplace.

When projecting your future aspirations or vision, you may reach for anything you want, but you can only experience what your chosen domain of glory possesses and thereby provides. Existence dictates experience. A Spirit/material existence is an open system of the cosmos and beyond – eternal and unlimited. The C/c domain and its experience embrace the Creator's everlasting Spirit and the Creator's revealed character in the temporal material realm.

If you want an everlasting journey across the universe and beyond, the Creator/cosmic human origin may be your option. Therefore, as you choose your human origin, you may select the glory characteristic powers the Creator/cosmic origin possesses as your Master of Ceremonies. It's the ultimate character enrichment for life and journey as you explore incredible mysteries in the now and beyond.

ALBERT EINSTEIN
"There are only two ways to live your life.
One is as though nothing is a miracle.
The other is as though everything is."

Please study "The Creator/cosmic Glory Driven Model Characteristics" in chapter four of the SDL text to enhance your understanding of its way of life. In the Creator/cosmic Human Origin Chart below, we will translate this description into a panoramic view of its implications for the human experience and journey. "It's the magic in the miracle." SDL text

On pages 54 – 57, you will discover the Creator/Cosmic Glory Driven Life Strategy as displayed in the Creator/Cosmic Chart of Human Origin. This Chart amplifies your cosmic glory characteristics and their impact on your life. In the Creator/Cosmic Glory Characteristics Domain of Existence, you discover who you are, how you live, and their implications regarding who you may become.

CREATOR/COSMIC (C/C) CHART OF HUMAN ORIGIN

The following characteristics, framing your identity, experience, and vision, will guide and enable your life decisions, directions, and lifestyle choices. Follow your guides!

DOMAIN OF EXISTENCE			
SPIRIT/MATERIAL DOMAIN – Spirit Eternal/Material Finite, Temporal. *Creator/cosmic (C/c) – A universe created/engineered with meaning and purpose.* ORIGIN DEFINES HUMAN CAPABILITIES From its Spirit/material domain, humans discover what they are (DOE), why they exist (COG), who they are (COB), and how they live (MOC). It's a C/c glory-driven life strategy.			
C/c CORE OF BEING *Who you are* COB Identity	C/c MASTER OF CEREMONIES *How you live* MOCs Experience	C/c PROCESSES OF BECOMING *Processes for living* MOCs Applied	C/c PERSONAL VISION FORECAST *Whom you become* Aspiration
Elevate Your Potential – GBA			
Intentionally Created Spirit/ material C/c Being. Chapter 1	<u>Strategic</u> C/c Glory MOC Characteristics for strategic guidance and empowerment. ***Creator's transcendent intentional Glory-driven will of filling the earth with His glory –*** *through glorifying living epistles.*	Your potential is dynamic as it merges aptitude, attitude, actions, and assignments! *Elevate your strategic, holistic potential through the C/c glory of intentionality with strategic planning and strategy –* in processes for performing *God's will of filling the earth with His glory characteristics* in your worth, meaning, purpose, and intentional life of worship, discipleship, and likeness.	Aspire to ***elevate your strategic potential of intentionality with plans and strategy to fulfill the Creator's glory-driven transcendent will of filling the earth with His glory*** *in a magnificent, glorifying universe – The heavens declare His glory. Don't let the heavens outperform the church.*
C/c Being of Phenomenal Potential Chapter 2	<u>Growth</u> C/c Glory MOC Characteristics ***Intentionality of Growth –*** *Transcend self-constraints by living beyond the limits of harmful feelings and conditions that discourage and defeat.*	Elevate your potential for increase (growth) by transcending self-constraints in C/c glory by mastering the art of stretching in the beyond arena—growing spiritually, personally, and professionally.	Aspire to ***intentionally elevate your growth potential by Stretching in the Beyond Arena,*** *transcending self-constraints – Becoming more than you can be*

C/c Being of Maturing Capability Chapter 3	Administrative C/c Glory MOC Characteristics *An Intentional Truth-driven life (run to the Truth) of Authorized Living* provides transcendent ideas for transcendent standards, maximizing maturity in authorized living. Standards measure maturity. Only transcendent standards produce peak human maturity.	*Elevate your potential for maturity in transcendent standards derived from the C/c glory of authority-driven behaviors.* Processes of authorized living in a truth-driven life generate transcendent standards of fulfillment in maturing ontology (existence/being), epistemology (knowledge), and teleology (purpose), linking maturity, responsibility, and authenticity. *The effectiveness of the standards constitutes the measure of maturity.*	Aspire to *intentionally elevate your maturing potential in a truth-driven life of authorized living* in transcendent standards that maximize maturity.

Design The Person You Want to Become

Being of Spirit/material Creator/cosmic glory Chapter 4	Essential C/c Glory MOC Characteristics *A C/c DOE Domain provides for a glory-driven life in a Sacred-driven Lifestyle of wholeness, meaning, and fulfillment.*	Design the person you want to become by embracing C/c glory characteristics as the essence of who you are and how you live. Engage processes for adopting a C/c glory-driven life of a sacred-driven lifestyle – *sacred nourishment* (wholeness), *sacred honor* (meaning), and *sacred life* (fulfillment). The sacred fills the earth with His glory.	Out of your chosen C/c DOE Domain, aspire to *design a Glory-driven life with a Sacred-driven Lifestyle* manifesting God's glory in whole-ness, meaning, and fulfill-ment for humanity and the cosmos.
Being of Creator/ cosmic Inspiration Chapter 5	Inspiration C/c Glory MOC Characteristics *Hope is born of faith and love. 1 Cor 13:13*	Design an inscribed passionate heart with C/c glory characteristics of inspiration for the person you want to become. Processes for writing in your heart – hope, faith, and love for an inspiring life	Out of your chosen C/c DOE Domain, aspire to *design an inscribed in-spiring heart of hope, faith, and love* for benefi-cial universal existence.

Being of Creator/ cosmic Intelligence Chapter 6	Intelligence–C/c Glory MOC Characteristics Hear **thoughts of God's character** as intelligent expressions of His heart-mind-spirit-aligned glory of Holy Wholeness – in resounding sounds, "there is no speech or language where their voice is not heard." (Psalm 19)	Design an intelligent mind of C/c glory character thoughts of aligned wholeness. Humility demonstrated is the mark of wholeness achieved. Intellectual wholeness acquired in gratitude, worship, and service processes may hear God's thoughts as character sounds of heart-mind alignment – All the law and the prophets hang on character thoughts of love (Mat 22: 37-40). Christ's mind in you as character thoughts of service in one accord (Ph 2:1-11). Both examples demonstrate heart and mind alignment. It's the unified intelligent sounds that C/c Glory speaks.	Out of your chosen C/c DOE Domain, **aspire to design a C/c character-driven uni ied intelligence of heart-mind-spirit-aligned wholeness** – ho-listic, integrated knowl-edge, including cosmic, majestic complexity. The measure of wholeness achieved prescribes hu-mility's potential and its accompanying dimension of acquired intelligence.

Define the Spirituality that Defines You

| C/c Spirit/ material Being. Chapter 7 | Meaning – C/c Glory MOC Characteristics

C/c Glory MOC Characteristic of Eternal Life is expressed in love, light, and life. Love without truth is not love at all, and truth without love is not the truth at all. Aligned Love and Truth are Life. | Define your C/c glory everlasting life spirituality of love, light, and life in Holy Oneness with enhanced reconciled human relationships, advanced knowledge of reality with beneficially aligned worldviews, and an everlasting and fulfilling life. | Aspire to define a **C/c glo-ry-driven spirituality of everlasting life** that is ever present in love, light, and life – beyond the material universe of death. |
| C/c Sacred Being Chapter 8 | Sacred – MOC Glory Characteristics

Value the Sacred
Holy human manifestations of C/c glory transition the sacred from its initial inanimate material form to its intended living form—the temple of God as living beings of worship. | Define the C/c sacred glory characteristics in temples of human flesh through worship, sacraments, rituals, pilgrimages, and life actions that value C/c sacred spirituality, developing the sacred as human sanctity with everlasting futures of peace. We cannot build a cathedral in every town, but we can build a cathedral in every heart. Religions live in cathedrals. God lives in human hearts – His living temple. | Aspire to **define a C/c glory-driven everlasting life spirituality as valued sacred cathedrals of God's dwelling places in every heart** – beyond cosmic material to human manifestations, giving humanity a great future. "As the sacred goes, so goes the world." SDL text |

C/c Relational Being Chapter 9	*Relational – C/c* Glory MOC Characteristics **Holy Wholeness** – Relational Wholeness – oneness in diversity .	Define your relational spirituality in C/c glory of lifelong serving relationships of wholeness, providing sacrificial behaviors of forgiveness and reconciliation for oneness in diversity .	Aspire to define ***a C/c Glory-driven everlasting life spirituality in lifelong serving relationships of wholeness*** – *beyond universal cosmic brokenness.*
C/c Community Being Chapter 10	*Community – MOC Glory Characteristics* ***Partnerships of love, light, and life*** *produce a transcendent Beyond Culture.* "I like living in a culturally Christian country… I call myself a cultural Christian" Richard Dawkins .	Define your spirituality as a community of holy oneness built on transcendent principles rather than power – a culture of *beyond partnerships in love that gives, light that guides, and life that grows. It's a spirit of one accord producing the Beyond Culture—spirit culture, Jesus' culture, and Sacred Culture.*	Aspire to ***define a C/c glory-driven "Beyond Culture" spirituality in partnerships of Love, light, and life*** *beyond cosmic material-driven self-interest divisionary associations.*
C/c Source defined Being Chapter 11	*Identity – C/c Glory MOC Characteristics* ***C/c Source-defined humanity of Everlasting Service***	*Define your being in a C/c Source-begotten life that transcends the material realm, projecting service that is better than self* in processes of "bless and bestow."	Aspire to ***define a C/c Source-driven Everlasting Serving Influence*** of "Bless and Bestow" – service that is better than self .

▶ *ACTION ITEM FOURTEEN: Specify meaningful Creator/cosmic Human Origin Chart observations. For increased comprehension, share these beneficial observations with others in your Discovery Group.*

On pages 58 - 68, you will discover the Empowerment of MOC Glory Characteristics – Be Glory Empowered in a Glory-filled Life.

C/c Glory-driven life Master of Ceremonies Strategy

Develop your Creator cosmic C/c MOC Glory-driven Life Strategy in each module. This workbook will build your C/c MOC strategy by characterizing its glory's implications in each chapter. Feel free to adjust the MOCs as you feel appropriate. This exercise aims to recognize the MOC influence gained from each model of human origin as applied to the life of each of its adherents. *The C/c Glory-driven Model, in its essential and applicational design, will facilitate man's chief end of glorifying God and enjoying Him forever (Ps 145).*

- Elevate Your Potential – C/c Glory-driven Life MOC Strategy
  - ▶ *Action Item*
- Design The Person You Want to Become – C/c Glory-driven Life MOC Strategy
  - ▶ *Action Item*
- Define The Spirituality That Defines You – C/c Glory-driven Life MOC Strategy
  - ▶ *Action Item*

Recently, well-known atheistic scientist Richard Dawkins told Rachel Johnson of LBC News.

"I like living in a culturally Christian country,
though I do not believe a single word of the Christian faith...
I call myself a cultural Christian. I'm not a believer,
but there's a distinction between being a believing Christian and a cultural Christian...
I love hymns and Christmas carols and sort of feel at home in the Christian ethos."

This remarkable statement from one who rejects belief in God is a resolute testimony of the cultural benefits the faith in Christ provides to humanity. It suggests a profound preference for a Christian cultural experience, as illustrated in the SDL choice of human origin. Richard Dawkins is to be commended for his transparent honesty—a laudable trait and an extolling example.

In selecting the Creator/cosmic (C/c) human origin, the Center of Gravity (COG), Core of Being (COB), and Master of Ceremonies (MOC) are aligned for your identity and experience in your Creator/cosmic world.

The combined Creator/cosmic-driven glory model provides the best of both worlds. It maximizes benefits and minimizes deficiencies. It is a visionary future with the extraordinary potential of hope beyond all limitations and terminations. It's your choice in everlasting life.

Your center of gravity domain determines your identity. Your master of ceremonies is the product of the domain's glory characteristics. From these expressions of the COG domain, your aspirations for life are framed. Processes are defined to facilitate your glory-driven life strategy.

The eleven Behavioral Objectives are embedded in the chart descriptions to provide a more precise definition of the journey you are projecting. The first Life Empowerment is employed in each chapter to enable effective goal accomplishment. As you work through each chapter in the chart, you will become who you want to be. Enjoy your chosen journey!

In building your vision, your selected goals give personal expression to your predefined realities. As projected in the SDL text, "Your vision of the future becomes the maturation of your view of the past." That is, human origin defines human futures. You can only become what your domain of existence allows.

The C/c MOCs reflect the character of the Creator and His essence of everlasting life. Consider four MOC glory characteristics that guided and empowered Jesus' journey – the Sacred, Holy Wholeness (oneness with the Father and Holy Spirit), Kingdom of God authority, and the Will of God.

Jesus gained victory over Lucifer through the sacred MOC. The sacred is the material manifestation of the holy. And since calvary humans as the temple of God manifest the holiness of God in the flesh as did Christ. The holy sacred always defeats evil and its strategies of iniquity—adherence to the sacred stops in its tracks wickedness in high places. Since Adam and Eve, sacred compromise has always been a resounding defeat.

The intentional will of God (MOC) to fill the earth with His glory took Christ to the cross and brought Him out of the grave. Even when you are seemingly dead or incapacitated in the trials of life, the MOC will of God prevails. When the final epitaph has been written, the MOC of everlasting life in the will of God rises above death with ultimate victory over that which seeks its demise. The stone always moves at the will of God, while the grave gives up what it could not hold. Victory is a core domain of C/c MOC characterizations. The more MOCs you embrace, the more the Creator's character of victory abides in you.

In worship and discipleship, MOCs live in you, granting you the capabilities of who they are. Embrace them with the wonder of magic in the miracle. Live with anticipation as they bring more than you can imagine to your journey. In C/c glory MOCs, you will discover God's manifest presence that will never leave you. God's elevating revelations of truth will enrich you. The powers of personal and corporate transformation will advance your journey. As Moses' life illustrates, the abiding presence of the glory of the Creator/cosmos suggests the ordinary should be concerned (look out), for the extraordinary may become commonplace.

MOCs are characteristic expressions of your COG and possess the powers of your human origin domain. In the Creator/cosmic origin, MOCs are unlimited and eternal as defined by their domain of existence. They represent the power of the universe and beyond. As embraced, they shape your life and journey with an impact that transforms you into their likeness. They become your potential for the future.

There is a three-step process for inscribing C/c MOC glory characteristics into your heart.

1. *Recognize* – <u>Value</u> their domain significance – adoration/worship.
2. *Replicate* – <u>Live</u> their influential capabilities – lifestyle/discipleship.
3. *Reproduce* – <u>Become</u> in your person the characteristics of their essence – likeness, intelligence, and life – an incarnational effect.

As you employ the below Creator/cosmic (C/c) glory MOC characteristics in the above-prescribed format, they will guide and enable your life decisions, directions, and lifestyle. The prescribed format includes, value as worship, living as discipleship, and becoming as likeness. In processes of worship, discipleship, and likeness, MOCs are continuously inscribed in your heart. What you write in your heart determines who you become and the life you experience. "For as he thinketh in his heart, so is he" (Proverbs 23:7).

This glory-inscribed heart shapes you with its likeness, knowledge, and transforming influence. Its presence as God's intimate (C/c) glory shapes you into His likeness. In your glory-shaped person, you become a portrayal of God – an incarnational effect, a living epistle. Its knowledge as an essential intellectual characteristic expression of God's (C/c) glory becomes a window into the broader domain of God's intelligence. His glory, as with the Trinity, is a unified essence that offers distinction yet commonality. These understanding insights of artistic richness into His glorious being must *always* align with the Biblical description. Its glorious life-transforming influence holistically changes you into His likeness in generational power so that you bring His overwhelming personal and beneficial influence to your world.

Follow inscribed MOCs to be Glory-Empowered!

CREATOR COSMIC
MASTER OF CEREMONIES IMPLEMENTATION

The following MOC characteristics in the prescribed format will guide and enable your life decisions, directions, and lifestyle choices. Follow to be empowered!

Elevate Your Potential – GBA			
Intentionally Created Spirit/material C/c Being. Chapter 1	Strategic C/c Glory MOC Characteristics for strategic guidance and empowerment. **Creator's transcendent intentional Glory-driven will of filling the earth with His glory** – *through glorifying living epistles.*	Your potential is dynamic as it merges aptitude, attitude, actions, and assignments! *Elevate your strategic, holistic potential through the C/c glory of intentionality with strategic planning and strategy* – in processes for performing *God's will of filling the earth with His glory characteristics* in your worth, meaning, purpose, and intentional life of worship, discipleship, and likeness.	Aspire to **elevate your strategic potential of intentionality with plans and strategy to fulfill the Creator's glory-driven transcendent will of filling the earth with His glory** *in a magnificent, glorifying universe – The heavens declare His glory. Don't let the heavens outperform the church.*
C/c Being of Phenomenal Potential Chapter 2	Growth C/c Glory MOC Characteristics **Intentionality of Growth** – *Transcend self-constraints by living beyond the limits of harmful feelings and conditions that discourage and defeat.*	Elevate your potential for increase (growth) by transcending self-constraints in C/c glory by mastering the art of stretching in the beyond arena—growing spiritually, personally, and professionally.	Aspire *to* **intentionally elevate your growth potential by Stretching in the Beyond Arena**, *transcending self-constraints – Becoming more than you can be*
C/c Being of Maturing Capability Chapter 3	Administrative C/c Glory MOC Characteristics **An Intentional Truth-driven life** *(run to the Truth)* **of Authorized Living** provides transcendent ideas for transcendent standards, maximizing maturity in authorized living. Standards measure maturity. Only transcendent standards produce peak human maturity.	*Elevate your potential for maturity in transcendent standards derived from the C/c glory of authority-driven behaviors.* Processes of authorized living in a truth-driven life generate transcendent standards of fulfillment in maturing ontology (existence/being), epistemology (knowledge), and teleology (purpose), linking maturity, responsibility, and authenticity. *The effectiveness of the standards constitutes the measure of maturity.*	Aspire to **intentionally elevate your maturing potential in a truth-driven life of authorized living** *in transcendent standards that maximize maturity.*

Module One: ELEVATE YOUR POTENTIAL – Through implementing your Creator/cosmic (C/c) glory MOC characteristics .

You will Elevate Your Potential as you employ the below Creator/cosmic (C/c) glory MOC characteristics. In the processes of worship, discipleship, and likeness, MOCs are inscribed in your heart. What you write in your heart determines who you become and the life you experience. "For as he thinketh in his heart, so is he" (Proverbs 23:7). This inscribed heart shapes you by inserting its likeness, knowledge, and transforming influence. *Follow inscribed MOCs to be Glory-Empowered!*

Please note that the MOCs inscribed in the heart bring to their recipient the presence of its MOC reality, the knowledge that the MOC reality possesses, and the transforming effect that the MOC reality provides. *This MOC presence, knowledge, and transformation is Glory-Empowerment!*

C/c Glory MOC characteristics for elevating your potential:

    <u>*Strategic C/c Glory MOC Characteristics*</u> – Creator's Intentional Will of a Glory-Filled Life for all Humanity

        Value – C/c The Intentional will of God – Worship

        Live – Intentionally – Lifestyle/Discipleship

        Be – Intentional – Likeness

    <u>*Performance C/c Glory MOC Characteristics*</u> – Grow by Stretching

        Value – C/c Growth by Stretching – Worship

        Live – Growingly – Lifestyle/Discipleship

        Be – Growing – Likeness

    <u>*Administrative C/c Glory MOC Characteristics*</u> – Embrace a Maturing Truth-driven Life for Authorized Living. Run to the Truth.

        Value – a C/c Maturing Truth-driven Life – Worship

        Live – a Maturing Truth-driven Lifestyle – Discipleship

        Be – a Maturing Truth-driven Authorized Life – Likeness

---

▶ *ACTION ITEM FIFTEEN: C/c Glory Elevating Potential – Inscribe the above <u>Life-Elevating</u> C/c Glory MOC characteristics in your heart. MOCs are written in your heart through adoration, lifestyle, and likeness, bringing presence, knowledge, and transforming influence – Creator/cosmic Glory Likeness. Share with your Discovery Group at least one impact these MOCs have on your life.*

Design The Person You Want to Become			
Being of Spirit/material Creator/cosmic glory Chapter 4	Essential C/c Glory MOC Characteristics *A C/c COG Domain provides for a glory-driven life in a Sacred-driven Lifestyle of wholeness, meaning, and fulfillment.*	Design the person you want to become by embracing C/c glory characteristics as the essence of who you are and how you live. Engage processes for adopting a C/c glory-driven life of a sacred-driven lifestyle – *sacred nourishment* (wholeness), *sacred honor* (meaning), and *sacred life* (fulfillment). The sacred fills the earth with His glory.	Out of your chosen C/c COG Domain, aspire to *design a Glory-driven life with a Sacred-driven Lifestyle* manifesting God's glory in wholeness, meaning, and fulfillment for humanity and the cosmos.
Being of Creator/cosmic Inspiration Chapter 5	Inspiration C/c Glory MOC Characteristics *Hope is born of faith and love.* *1 Cor 13:13*	Design an inscribed passionate heart with C/c glory characteristics of inspiration for the person you want to become. Processes for writing in your heart – hope, faith, and love for an inspiring life	Out of your chosen C/c COG Domain, aspire to *design an inscribed inspiring heart of hope, faith, and love* for beneficial universal existence.
Being of Creator/cosmic Intelligence Chapter 6	Intelligence–C/c Glory MOC Characteristics Hear **thoughts of God's character** *as intelligent expressions of His heart-mind-spirit-aligned glory of Holy Wholeness – in resounding sounds, "there is no speech or language where their voice is not heard."(Psalm 19)*	Design an intelligent mind of C/c glory character thoughts of aligned wholeness . Humility demonstrated is the mark of wholeness achieved . Intellectual wholeness acquired in gratitude, worship, and service processes may hear *God's thoughts as character sounds of heart-mind alignment –* All the law and the prophets hang on character thoughts of love (Mat 22: 37-40) . Christ's mind in you as character thoughts of service in one accord (Ph 2:1-11) . Both examples demonstrate heart and mind alignment . *It's the unified intelligent sounds that C/c Glory speaks.*	Out of your chosen C/c COG Domain, *aspire to design a C/c character-driven unified intelligence of heart-mind-spirit-aligned wholeness –* holistic, integrated knowledge, including cosmic, majestic complexity . *The measure of wholeness achieved prescribes humility's potential and its accompanying dimension of acquired intelligence.*

Module Two: DESIGN THE PERSON YOU WANT TO BECOME – Through implementing your Creator/cosmic (C/c) glory MOC characteristics .

You will Design the Person You Want to Become as you employ the Creator/cosmic (C/c) glory MOC characteristics below. In the processes of worship, discipleship, and likeness, MOCs are inscribed in your heart. What you write in your heart determines who you become and the life you experience. "For as he thinketh in his heart, so is he" (Proverbs 23:7). This inscribed heart of MOC glory shapes you by inserting its likeness, knowledge, and transforming influence. *Follow inscribed MOCs to be Glory-Empowered!*

Please note that the MOCs inscribed in the heart bring to their recipient the presence of its MOC reality, the knowledge that the MOC reality possesses, and the transforming effect that the MOC reality provides. *This likeness, knowledge, and transforming effect is Glory-Empowerment!*

C/c Glory MOC characteristics for designing the person you want to become:

    C/c Glory-driven Life – MOC Characteristics – A Sacred C/c Glory-driven Life – the temple, dwelling place of God.

        Value – a C/c Sacred Glory-driven Life – Worship

        Live – a Sacred Glory-driven Lifestyle – Discipleship

        Be – a Sacred Glory-driven Person – Likeness

    Inspiring MOC Characteristics – A C/c Glory-driven Heart

        Value – an Inscribed C/c Hope-filled Heart of C/c Glory – Worship

        Live – an Inscribed Hope-filled Heart Lifestyle – Discipleship

        Be – an Inscribed Hope-filled Heart – Likeness

    Intelligent MOC Characteristics – A C/c Glory-driven Mind

        Value – Intelligent Thoughts of C/c Glory – Adore/Worship

        Live – Intelligent Rational lifestyle of C/c Glory – Discipleship

        Be – C/c Glory Intelligence – Likeness

        God's Mind and Heart are always aligned = His Intelligence

---

▶ *ACTION ITEM SIXTEEN: C/c Glory Designing Possibilities – Inscribe the above* <u>Life-Shaping</u> *C/c Glory MOC characteristics in your heart. MOCs are written in your heart through worship, discipleship, and likeness, bringing presence and knowledge and transforming influence – Creator/cosmic Glory Likeness. Share with your Discovery Group at least one impact these MOCs have on your life.*

Define the Spirituality that Defines You

C/c Spirit/material Being. Chapter 7	*Meaning* – *C/c Glory MOC Characteristics* **C/c Glory MOC Characteristic of Eternal Life** *is expressed in love, light, and life. Love without truth is not love at all, and truth without love is not the truth at all. Aligned Love and Truth are Life.*	Define your C/c glory everlasting life spirituality of love, light, and life in Holy Oneness with enhanced reconciled human relationships, advanced knowledge of reality with beneficially aligned worldviews, and an everlasting and fulfilling life.	Aspire to define a **C/c glory-driven spirituality of everlasting life** *that is ever present in love, light, and life – beyond the material universe of death.*
C/c Sacred Being Chapter 8	*Sacred* – *MOC Glory Characteristics* **Value the Sacred** *Holy human manifestations of C/c glory transition the sacred from its initial inanimate material form to its intended living form—the temple of God as living beings of worship.*	Define the C/c sacred glory characteristics in temples of human flesh through worship, sacraments, rituals, pilgrimages, and life actions that value C/c sacred spirituality, developing the sacred as human sanctity with everlasting futures of peace. *We cannot build a cathedral in every town, but we can build a cathedral in every heart.* Religions live in cathedrals. God lives in human hearts – His living temple.	Aspire to **define a C/c glory-driven everlasting life spirituality as valued sacred cathedrals of God's dwelling places in every heart** – *beyond cosmic material to human manifestations, giving humanity a great future.* "As the sacred goes, so goes the world." SDL text
C/c Relational Being Chapter 9	*Relational* – *C/c Glory MOC Characteristics* **Holy Wholeness** – Relational Wholeness – oneness in diversity.	Define your relational spirituality in C/c glory of lifelong serving relationships of wholeness, providing sacrificial behaviors of forgiveness and reconciliation for oneness in diversity.	Aspire to define **a C/c Glory-driven everlasting life spirituality in lifelong serving relationships of wholeness** – *beyond universal cosmic brokenness.*
C/c Community Being Chapter 10	*Community* – *MOC Glory Characteristics* **Partnerships of love, light, and life** produce a transcendent Beyond Culture. "I like living in a culturally Christian country... I call myself a cultural Christian" Richard Dawkins.	Define your spirituality as a community of holy oneness built on transcendent principles rather than power – a culture of *beyond partnerships in love that gives, light that guides, and life that grows. It's a spirit of one accord producing the Beyond Culture— spirit culture, Jesus' culture, and Sacred Culture.*	Aspire to **define a C/c glory-driven "Beyond Culture" spirituality in partnerships of Love, light, and life** *beyond cosmic material-driven self-interest divisionary associations.*
C/c Source defined as Being Chapter 11	*Identity* – *C/c Glory MOC Characteristics* **C/c Source-defined humanity of Everlasting Service**	*Define your being in a C/c Source-begotten life that transcends the material realm, projecting service that is better than self in processes of "bless and bestow."*	Aspire to **define a C/c Source-driven Everlasting Serving Influence** of *"bless and bestow" – service that is better than self.*

Module Three: DEFINE THE SPIRITUALITY THAT DEFINES YOU – Through Implementing your chosen Creator/cosmic C/c MOCs .

As you employ the below Creator/cosmic (C/c) glory MOC characteristics that define your spirituality, this spirituality will define you. In the processes of worship, discipleship, and likeness, MOCs are inscribed in your heart. What you write in your heart determines who you become and the life you experience. "For as he thinketh in his heart, so is he" (Proverbs 23:7). This inscribed heart of MOC glory shapes you by inserting its likeness, knowledge, and transforming influence. *Follow inscribed MOCs to be Glory-Empowered!*

Please note that the MOCs inscribed in the heart bring to their recipient the presence of its MOC reality, the knowledge that the MOC reality possesses, and the transforming effect that the MOC reality provides. *This presence, knowledge, and transforming effect is Glory-Empowerment!*

C/c MOC Glory characteristics for defining the spirituality that defines you:

> <u>*C/c Glory MOC Characteristics of Spirituality*</u> – A C/c Glory-driven spirituality
>> *Value – C/c Everlasting Life (Love, Light, Life) – Worship*
>> *Live – Everlasting Life Lifestyle (Love, Light, Life) – Discipleship*
>> *Be – Everlasting Life (Love, Light, Life) – Likeness*
>
> <u>*C/c Glory MOC Sacred Characteristics of Spirituality*</u> – A C/c Glory-driven Sacred Spirituality (Please note that in the New Testament, the temple transitioned from a material dwelling to a living dwelling – the people of God. As Christians, humans in this world are the intended living *sacred* dwelling place of God)
>> *Value – Sacred Manifestations of C/c glory – Reverence/Worship*
>> *Live – a Sacred Lifestyle – Discipleship*
>> *Be – a Sacred Life – Likeness*
>
> <u>*C/c Glory MOC Relational Characteristics of Spirituality*</u> – Holy Wholeness (Oneness) – Lifelong Serving Relationships
>> *Value – Relational Wholeness (Holy Oneness) – Reverence/Worship*
>> *Live – Relational Wholeness Lifestyle – Discipleship*
>> *Be – Relationally Whole – Likeness*
>
> <u>*C/c Glory MOC Community Characteristics of Spirituality*</u> – Partnerships of Love, Light, and Life – Peace in One Accord
>> *Value – Partnerships of Everlasting Life (Love, Light, and Life) – Reverence/Worship*
>> *Live – as Partnership of Everlasting Life Lifestyle (Love, Light, and Life) – Discipleship*
>> *Be – an Everlasting Life Partner in (Love, Light, and Life) – Likeness*
>
> <u>*C/c Glory MOC Source Characteristics of Spirituality*</u> – A C/c Source-begotten life
>> *Value – Source as the Creator – Worship*
>> *Live – Source in His Lifestyle – Discipleship*

Be – a Source Embodied Humanity (The Temple of God) – Likeness – We cannot build a cathedral in every town, but we can build a cathedral in every heart.

▶ *ACTION ITEM SEVENTEEN: C/c Glory Defining Spirituality – Inscribe the above <u>Life-Enriching</u> C/c Glory MOC characteristics in your heart. MOCs are written in your heart through worship, discipleship, and likeness, bringing presence and knowledge and transforming influence—Creator/cosmic Glory Likeness. Share with your Discovery Group at least one impact these MOCs have on your life.*

Now, you are ready to build your Creator/Cosmic Glory-Driven SDL Vision as presented in pages 69-80. In this visionary strategy, you will merge a glory-driven strategic *plan* with a glory-driven strategic *strategy*, shaping your future *aspirations* accomplished through SMART *goals* for achieving your *visionary design*.

CREATOR COSMIC GLORY MASTER OF CEREMONIES
A Creator/cosmic Character-Driven Life

▶ Be Intentional – Transcendent Intentionality – A Glory-filled Life

▶ Be More – Transcendent Growth – Stretch Beyond Constraints

▶ Be Distinguished – Transcendent Maturity – A Truth-driven Life of Authorized Living

▶ Be Discerning – Glory-Driven Life – Sacred-Driven Lifestyle

▶ Be Inspired – Inscribed Inspiring Heart – Hope, Faith, and Love

▶ Be Intelligent – Holistic Intelligence – Aligned Heart and Mind

▶ Be Spiritual – Everlasting Life Spirituality – Love, Light, and Life

▶ Be Greatness – Sacred Glory – Set-apart Glory-Driven Human Heart Cathedral

▶ Be Holy – Relational Wholeness – Oneness

▶ Be Unmeasurable – Partnerships of – Love, Light, and Life

▶ Be Legacy – Spirit/material Source Being – Everlasting Serving Influence

If you wish to employ other Creator/cosmic characteristics as your MOC, please feel free to use its guidance in your life . For validity, ensure that it exists in your chosen domain of origin . You can only experience what your domain of origin possesses .

CREATOR COSMIC GLORY DRIVEN LIFE
VISIONARY STRATEGY

The workbook will assist you in building your visionary strategy by providing characterizations from the text regarding MOC's future implications. Feel free to adjust the strategy as you feel appropriate. This exercise aims to recognize the visionary influence gained from each model of human origin as applied to the life of each of its adherents. The related goals and steps for accomplishments are personal to you and applied at your discretion – Best wishes for a great future.

- Elevate Your Potential – C/c Glory-driven Visionary Life Strategy
  - ▶ *Action Item*
- Design The Person You Want to Become – C/c Glory-driven Visionary Life Strategy
  - ▶ Action Item
- Define The Spirituality That Defines You – C/c Glory-driven Visionary Life Strategy
  - ▶ Action Item

Celebrate your achievements as they facilitate your SDL visionary progress.
Each chapter will give three components that shape your life and vision.

- Your C/c Glory – MOC for guidance and empowerment
- Your C/c Glory – Strategic Plan in your Behavioral Objective
- Your C/c Glory – Strategic Strategy in your aspirations as noted in your Human Origin Charts

VISIONARY MODULE ONE – Build your vision to Elevate Your Potential. As you fill in the descriptions below, your vision will become clear, empowered, and fulfilled. As always, it's the product of who you choose to become based on your choice of origin and its definition of who you are.

ELEVATE YOUR VISIONARY POTENTIAL – C/c SDL Visionary Life Strategy
Chapter One:
C/c Glory MOC – Be Intentional – Become your chosen C/c Glory-filled Life Characteristics
Processes for being intentional – plan and strategy.
  Behavioral Objective – Strategic Plan
  Build your SDL vision as an empowered, intentional C/c glory-driven life
  Aspiration – Strategic Strategy
  Elevate your transcendent strategic potential by living as your chosen C/c Glory Characteristics thereby filling the earth with the glory of God.

Life Empowerment – for strategic achievements.

Celebrate Calculated Achievements!

Set goals for living your chosen C/c Glory Characteristics as the person you want to become. Gain insight from chapter one in the Creator/cosmic Chart of Human Origin.

SMART Goal 1 –

_____

Specify steps to accomplish your goal.

1. _____

2. _____

3. _____

Celebrate each step's achievement!

Record in your journal – How, with whom, and where.

SMART Goal 2.

_____

Specify steps to accomplish your goal.

1. _____

2. _____

3. _____

Celebrate each step's achievement!

Record in your journal – How, with whom, and where.

Employ more goals if needed.

In your journal, record your progress. Then celebrate!

Chapter Two:

C/c Glory MOC – Be More – Stretch beyond constraints in the Beyond Arena

Processes for Growing!

Behavioral Objective – Strategic Plan

Grow to become more than you can be – transcend self-constraints.

Aspiration – Strategic Strategy

Elevate your strategic potential for transcendent Growth by Mastering the art of stretching.

Life Empowerment – for strategic accomplishments.

Stretch in the Beyond Arena

Celebrate calculated achievements!

Set goals for elevating your growing C/c potential by *Mastering the Art of Stretching*. Gain insight from chapter two in the Creator/cosmic Chart of Human Origin.

SMART Goal 1 –

_____

Specify steps to accomplish your goal.

1. _____

2. _____

3. _____

Celebrate each step's achievement!

Record in your journal – How, with whom, and where.

SMART Goal 2.

_____

Specify steps to accomplish your goal.

1. _____

2. _____

3. _____

Celebrate each step's achievement!

Record in your journal – How, with whom, and where.

Employ more goals if needed.

In your journal, record your progress. Then celebrate!

Chapter Three:

C/c Glory MOC – Be Distinguished – Assume Responsibility for a Truth-driven Life

Processes for maturing Distinction!

Behavioral Objective – Strategic Plan

Become a person of maturing distinction.

Aspiration – Strategic Strategy

     Elevate your strategic potential of maturity by engaging C/c glory characteristics in a Truth-driven life of Authorized living, applied to the five leadership keys for success.

Life Empowerment – for strategic accomplishments.

     Assume responsibility for life and mission.

     Celebrate calculated achievements!

Set goals for gaining a maturing distinction by responsibly employing transcendent standards of authorized living including the five, chapter three, leadership keys. Gain insight from chapter three in the Creator/cosmic Chart of Human Origin.

SMART Goal 1 –

_____

Specify steps to accomplish your goal.

1. _____

2. _____

3. _____

Celebrate each step's achievement!

     Record in your journal – How, with whom, and where.

SMART Goal 2.

_____

Steps for implementing the above effective processes for accomplishing your goal.

1. _____

2. _____

3. _____

Celebrate each step's achievement!

     Record in your journal – How, with whom, and where.

Employ more goals if needed.

     In your journal, record your progress. Then celebrate!

▶ *ACTION ITEM EIGHTEEN: Accomplish your above Visionary Performance Goals for Elevating Your C/c Glory-driven Potential by achieving the steps you have set for their fulfillment. Celebrate your achievements with those who share your life's journey. Record when, where, and who attended and any specific action they took to commemorate your achievement.*

DESIGN THE PERSON YOU WANT TO BECOME – C/c SDL Visionary Life Strategy

<u>Chapter Four:</u>

C/c Glory MOC – Be Discerning – Choose your C/c Glory-driven life in a Sacred Lifestyle

Processes for becoming C/c glory-driven sacred life!

    Behavioral Objective – Strategic Plan

        Become a person of value with meaning and purpose – Become Significant!

    Aspiration – Strategic Strategy

        Become a person of wholeness, meaning, and fulfillment in a Glory-driven Life with a Sacred-driven Lifestyle

    Life Empowerment – for strategic accomplishments.

        The power of choice

        Celebrate calculated achievements!

Set goals for designing your glory-driven life with a sacred-driven lifestyle through *sacred nourishment (wholeness), honor (meaning), and life (fulfillment)*. Gain insight from chapter four in the Creator/cosmic Chart of Human Origin.

SMART Goal 1 –

_____

Specify steps to accomplish your goal.

1. _____

2. _____

3. _____

Celebrate each step's achievement!

    Record in your journal – How, with whom, and where.

SMART Goal 2.

_____

Specify steps to accomplish your goal.

1. _____

2. _____

3. _____

Celebrate each step's achievement!

    Record in your journal – How, with whom, and where.

Employ more goals if needed.

    In your journal, record your progress. Then celebrate!

Chapter Five:

C/c Glory MOC – Be Inspired – Choose your C/c glory characteristics

Processes for inscribed heart inspirations!

    Behavioral Objective – **Strategic Plan**

        Inscribe (write) in your heart your chosen glory characteristics as the core of who you are.

    Aspiration – **Strategic Strategy**

        Light up your world with Hope – the passion of your C/c Glory MOCs inscribed in your heart as the place where you live.

    Life Empowerment – for strategic accomplishments.

        Passion from an inscribed heart

        Celebrate calculated achievements!

Set goals for inscribing your heart with faith, hope, and love. Gain insight from chapter five in the Creator/cosmic Chart of Human Origin.

SMART Goal 1 –

_____

Specify steps to accomplish your goal.

1. _____

2. _____

3. _____

Celebrate each step's achievement!

    Record in your journal – How, with whom, and where.

SMART Goal 2.

_____

    Specify steps to accomplish your goal.

1. _____

2. _____

3. _____

Celebrate each step's achievement!

    Record in your journal – How, with whom, and where.

Employ more goals if needed.

    In your journal, record your progress. Then celebrate!

Chapter Six:

C/c Glory MOC – Be Intelligent – Become holistic aligned C/c Intelligence

Processes for C/c Intelligence!

   Behavioral Objective – Strategic Plan

      Design your mind (hear, learn, think) as the intelligent thought your chosen glory conveys.

   Aspiration – Strategic Strategy

      Design a C/c glory/character-driven unified intelligence of spirit-heart-mind-aligned wholeness.

   Life Empowerment – for strategic accomplishments.

      Listen to the music

      Celebrate calculated achievements!

Set goals for designing the person of holistic aligned intelligence you want to become with *the sounds of C/c glory characteristics* – Gain insight from chapter six in the Creator/cosmic Chart of Human Origin.

SMART Goal 1 –

_____

Specify steps to accomplish your goal.

1. _____

2. _____

3. _____

Celebrate each step's achievement!

   Record in your journal – How, with whom, and where.

SMART Goal 2.

_____

Specify steps to accomplish your goal.

1. _____

2. _____

3. _____

Celebrate each step's achievement!

   Record in your journal – How, with whom, and where.

Employ more goals if needed.

   In your journal, record your progress. Then celebrate!

> ▶ *ACTION ITEM NINETEEN: Accomplish your above Visionary Personal Design Goals for Becoming The C/c Glory-driven Person You Want to Become by achieving the steps you have set for their fulfillment. Celebrate your achievements with those who share your life's journey. Record when, where, and who attended and any specific action they took to commemorate your achievement.*

DEFINE THE SPIRITUALITY THAT DEFINES YOU – C/c SDL Visionary Life Strategy

<u>Chapter Seven:</u>

C/c Glory MOC – Be Spiritual – Become C/c Everlasting Life Spirituality

Processes for becoming everlasting life!

   Behavioral Objective – Strategic Plan

      Become the C/c glory-driven spirituality that defines you.

   Aspiration – Strategic Strategy

      Define the C/c Glory-driven Everlasting Life Spirituality that defines you in love, light, and life.

   Life Empowerment – for strategic accomplishments.

      Wind beneath your wings

      Celebrate calculated achievements!

   Set goals for defining the *Everlasting Life Spirituality* that defines you in *deeds of love, light, and life* – Gain insight from chapter seven in the Creator/cosmic Chart of Human Origin.

SMART Goal 1 –

_____

Specify steps to accomplish your goal.

1. _____

2. _____

3. _____

Celebrate each step's achievement!

   Record in your journal – How, with whom, and where.

SMART Goal 2.

_____

Specify steps to accomplish your goal.

1. _____

2. _____

3. _____

Celebrate each step's achievement!

Record in your journal – How, with whom, and where.

Employ more goals if needed.

In your journal, record your progress. Then celebrate!

Chapter Eight:

C/c Glory MOC – Be Greatness – Become Sacred Manifestations of Everlasting Life Spirituality.

Processes for human manifestations of C/c glory!

Behavioral Objective – Strategic Plan

Give your world a great future –your strategic imperative of valuing the C/c sacred.

Aspiration – Strategic Strategy

Become a C/c Glory-driven spirituality of everlasting life sacred cathedrals – God's dwelling place in every heart.

Life Empowerment – for strategic accomplishments.

Value the sacred

Celebrate calculated achievements!

Set goals for defining the C/c *Sacred Cathedral* that defines you – *as living epistles or Temples of God – human manifestations of everlasting life* – Gain insight from chapter eight in the Creator/cosmic Chart of Human Origin.

SMART Goal 1 –

_____

Specify steps to accomplish your goal.

1. _____

2. _____

3. _____

Celebrate each step's achievement!

Record in your journal – How, with whom, and where.

SMART Goal 2.

_____

Specify steps to accomplish your goal.

1. _____

2. _____

3. _____

Celebrate each step's achievement!

    Record in your journal – How, with whom, and where.

Employ more goals if needed.

    In your journal, record your progress. Then celebrate!

Chapter Nine:

C/c Glory MOC – Be Holy – Relational Oneness in everlasting life spiritual relationships.

Processes for Holy Relationships – Oneness in everlasting life spiritual relationships!

    Behavioral Objective – Strategic Plan

        Become an instrument of peace in Holy Wholeness – Oneness.

    Aspiration – Strategic Strategy

        Create life-long serving relationships as Holy Wholeness in everlasting life spirituality.

    Life Empowerment – for strategic accomplishments.

      The power of one

    Celebrate calculated achievements!

Set goals for practicing the C/c *Holy Wholeness* of everlasting life spirituality – *long-term serving relationships* – Gain insight from chapter nine in the Creator/cosmic Chart of Human Origin.

SMART Goal 1 –

_____

Specify steps to accomplish your goal.

1. _____

2. _____

3. _____

Celebrate each step's achievement!

    Record in your journal – How, with whom, and where.

SMART Goal 2.

_____

Specify steps to accomplish your goal.

1. _____

2. _____

3. _____

Celebrate each step's achievement!

Record in your journal – How, with whom, and where.

Employ more goals if needed.

In your journal, record your progress. Then celebrate!

Chapter Ten:

C/c Glory MOC – Be Unmeasurable – Partners in a Love, Light, and Life culture.

Processes for building a Beyond Culture of Everlasting Life partnerships!

Behavioral Objective – Strategic Plan

Build a Beyond Culture of Partnerships in Love, Light, and Life – One Accord

Aspiration – Strategic Strategy

Build your Community with Everlasting Life Spirituality of Partnerships of Love, Light, and Life.

Life Empowerment – for strategic accomplishments.

Exponential power levels

Celebrate calculated achievements!

Set goals for employing the C/c *Everlasting Life Partnership Spirituality* that defines you – *in partnerships of love that gives, light that guides, and life that grows* – Gain insight from chapter ten in the Creator/cosmic Chart of Human Origin.

SMART Goal 1 –

_____

Specify steps to accomplish your goal.

1. _____

2. _____

3. _____

Celebrate each step's achievement!

Record in your journal – How, with whom, and where.

SMART Goal 2.

_____

Specify steps to accomplish your goal.

1. _____

2. _____

3. _____

Celebrate each step's achievement!

Record in your journal – How, with whom, and where.

Employ more goals if needed.

In your journal, record your progress. Then celebrate!

Chapter Eleven:

C/c Glory MOC – Be Legacy – Become C/c Source embodied, everlasting life spirituality. Processes for a Source-embodied spiritual humanity of everlasting life!

Behavioral Objective – Strategic Plan

Maximize Source-driven stewardship that matures Source-defined influence.

Aspiration – Strategic Strategy

Engage the seven processes of source-defined Everlasting Life influence.

Life Empowerment – for strategic accomplishments.

The power in your serve

Celebrate calculated achievements!

Set goals for becoming an Everlasting Life Service Spirituality – *employ the Source-defined influential processes* – Gain insight from chapter eleven in the Creator/cosmic Chart of Human Origin.

SMART Goal 1 –

_____

Specify steps to accomplish your goal.

1. _____

2. _____

3. _____

Celebrate each step's achievement!

Record in your journal – How, with whom, and where.

SMART Goal 2.

_____

Specify steps to accomplish your goal.

1. _____

2. _____

3. _____

Celebrate each step's achievement!

Record in your journal – How, with whom, and where.

Employ more goals if needed.

In your journal, record your progress. Then celebrate!

▶ *ACTION ITEM TWENTY: Accomplish your above Spiritual Goals for Your C/c Glory-driven Visionary Spirituality by achieving the steps you have set for their fulfillment. Celebrate your achievements with those who share your life's journey. Record when, where, and who attended and any specific action they took to commemorate your achievement.*

Congratulations!

You Have Completed Your Creator/cosmic SDL Glory-Driven Vision!

Your vision is specified in your goals and steps of achievement. With the empowerment of your MOCs and the projection of your aspirations for life, you are well-suited to engage your future with confidence and commitment. Keep your journal active, recording significant accomplishments that demonstrate your journey in your newly acquired capabilities of vision and MOC energies. It is your life envisioned and empowered to perform.

CHOOSE YOUR PREFERRED HUMAN ORIGIN

Selected Human Origin Becomes Your Personal Glory-Driven Life Strategy!

Your choice of human origin becomes your empowered, intentional, glory-driven life strategy. THANK YOU for taking the Strategic Driven Life Journey. I hope it has helped you navigate your world with greater confidence and energy. Strangely enough, tomorrow can be seen from the past you select as your starting point. It's the Cosmic or Creator/cosmic story – the origin determines destiny.

With the empowerment of your MOCs and the projection of your visionary aspirations for life, you are well-suited to engaging your future with confidence and commitment. Keep your journal active, recording significant accomplishments that demonstrate your journey in your newly acquired capabilities of vision and MOC energies. It is your life envisioned and empowered to perform.

Please initial your chosen life option.

A cosmic life option _____

A Creator/cosmic life option _____

Very Best Wishes for a Great Future.

E. Derel Peterson

Strategic Driven Life Journal

_____

_____

_____

_____

_____

_____

_____

_____

_____

_____

_____

_____

_____

_____

_____

_____

_____

_____

_____

_____

_____

_____

_____

_____

_____

_____

_____

_____

_____

_____

Strategic Driven Life Journal

Strategic Driven Life Journal